Praise for *8 Simple Tool*

D0446121

Dr. Todd Cartmell has an amazing gift
of parenting seem doable. *8 Simple To*
practical, easy to read, heartwarming,
a proven game plan for raising healthy kids who will grow up to be
adults—and this is it!

> —ARLENE PELLICANE, author, *31 Days to Becoming a Happy Mom* and
> *Growing Up Social*

Todd Cartmell's book is loaded with practical, useful tips and powerful
insights that empower parents to repair and strengthen family relationships.
This book is a "must read" not only for those seeking help in navigating the
challenges of parenthood, but for anyone needing more tools in their work
with children.

> —LINDA MICHEL, early childhood educator, learning behavior specialist,
> mother

Dr. Cartmell provides a tremendous resource for parents of every experience
level. Better than simply being a good read with helpful insights, *8 Simple
Tools for Raising Great Kids* will undoubtedly be a go-to reference time and
again providing clear, easily applied solutions to difficult parenting challenges.
Families using these tools will enjoy long-term strength and health in their
relationships.

> —REV. RANDY ISOLA, children's pastor, Christ Community Church,
> St. Charles, Illinois

Simple tools? When I looked at the title of Dr. Cartmell's book and the list of
tools he includes, I thought the title was misleading. Listening isn't simple.
Correcting isn't simple. It's not easy to connect today either. Then I read the
book and understood the title. I agree with it. Totally. Todd absolutely makes
these tools simple! The number of practical and realistic details in short,
accessible chapters is impressive. His stories make them come alive. His
analogies are rich. Did you know you can be a gold miner and play catch all
day? Your children are like dump trucks and cereal boxes? I agree! Use Todd's
ideas and you'll gain confidence. Your children will notice your new heart for
them and your relationships will be healthier than ever. Read this book now!

> —KATHY KOCH, PhD, president and founder of Celebrate Kids, Inc., and
> author of *Screens and Teens*, *No More Perfect Kids*, and *8 Great Smarts*

What a concept! A book for moms and dads that's fun to read. With lots of fresh wisdom and welcome encouragement.

—JAY PAYLEITNER, conference speaker and bestselling author of *52 Things Kids Need from a Dad* and *What If God Wrote Your Bucket List?*

Todd Cartmell has crafted a fabulous go-to manual for parents in *8 Simple Tools for Raising Great Kids*. Full of relevant examples, helpful advice, and practical tips, this book will empower you to build solid relationships with your kids and strengthen your family bond.

—KAREN EHMAN, *New York Times* bestselling author and Proverbs 31 Ministries speaker. Wife and mom of three.

There's nothing simple about parenting, but it's certainly easier if you are equipped for the job! Todd Cartmell knows what parents need and he's shared it on the pages of this book. I'm grateful for such a practical, easy-to-read resource for parents!

—JILL SAVAGE, mom of five, coauthor of *No More Perfect Kids*

As a parent, I am interested in people formation (relationally, spiritually, and physically) more than rule-focused behavior. As a professor and clinician, I am always looking for resources to supplement my work with parents. Dr. Cartmell satisfies both of these needs for me with a wonderful resource in his *8 Simple Tools for Raising Great Kids*. In this book he provides skills and a relational philosophy for parents raising kids in our contemporary society. He emphasizes relational truths of parenting clearly and through excellent metaphors. I especially enjoyed the playing catch metaphor, which focuses us on participating with our children. This is a resource I will encourage my graduate students in marriage and family therapy to provide for parents in the clinic and through parenting groups at their churches.

—DAVID J. VAN DYKE, associate professor, Marriage & Family Therapy Program, Wheaton College

8 SIMPLE TOOLS FOR RAISING GREAT KIDS

DR. TODD CARTMELL

MOODY PUBLISHERS

CHICAGO

All Scripture quotations, unless otherwise indicated, are taken from the Holy Bible, New International Version®, NIV®. Copyright © 1973, 1978, 1984, 2011 by Biblica, Inc.™ Used by permission of Zondervan. All rights reserved worldwide. www.zondervan.com. The "NIV" and "New International Version" are trademarks registered in the United States Patent and Trademark Office by Biblica, Inc.™

Published in association with the literary agency of Transatlantic Agency.

Edited by Pam Pugh
Interior design: Ragont Design
Cover design: Christopher Tobias, Tobias Design
Cover photo of children on dock copyright © 2013 by Angela Lumsden/Stocksy (62598). All rights reserved.
Author photo: Julie Salzmann

Library of Congress Cataloging-in-Publication Data

Cartmell, Todd
  8 simple tools for raising great kids / Todd Cartmell.
      pages cm
  Summary: "Written in conversational style with plenty of real-life examples, child psychologist Todd Cartmell offers parents and others who care for children workable ideas for enriching everyday life and growing healthy children under the categories of talking, listening, influencing, connecting, teaching, encouraging, correcting, leading"—Provided by publisher.
  ISBN 978-0-8024-1387-1 (paperback)
  1. Child rearing. 2. Parenting. I. Title. II. Title: Eight simple tools for raising great kids.
  HQ769.C34144 2016
  306.874--dc23
                        2015029995

The names and details of the children, families, and situations described in this book have been significantly changed and/or presented in composite form, in order to provide the reader with illustrations of actual experiences while ensuring the absolute privacy of the many children, teens, and parents the author has been privileged to work with for over twenty years. Any resemblance of these composite illustrations to any actual person is entirely coincidental.

This book is not intended to be a substitute for professional evaluation and treatment. If you have significant concerns about your child's behavioral or emotional functioning, please consult with a qualified mental health professional.

To all the parents I have known
who work tirelessly in raising the wonderful children
that God has given them.

Contents

Foreword   9

Introduction   11

Tool #1: Talking

Control Your Volume Knob   17

If Unsure, Press Pause   21

Start with You   25

Be Easy to Listen To   29

Play a Game of Catch   33

Tool #2: Listening

Listen First   39

Listen to Understand   43

Listen Often   47

Listen to Everything   51

Listen with Your Entire Body   55

Tool #3: Influencing

Remember Who They Are   61

Understand the Power of Your Words   65

Be a Fountain of Life   69

See More Than Meets the Eye   73

Find the Lesson   77

Tool #4: Connecting

Use Your Touch   83

Avoid the Time Trap   87

Get into Their World   91

Learn Together   95

Have a Regular Family Time   99

Tool #5: Teaching

Emphasize Respect   105
Practice Positive Behavior   109
Teach Flexible Thinking   113
Find the Solution   117
Solve Problems on the Spot   121

Tool #6: Encouraging

Point Out Positive Behaviors   127
Point Out Positive Traits   131
Water the *Whole* Lawn Regularly   135
Look Past the Failure   139
Look Backward Together   143

Tool #7: Correcting

Focus on Your Job   149
Help Your Kids Bounce   153
Make a Quick Response   157
Teach the Right Lesson   161
Teach the Right Lesson the Right Way   165

Tool #8: Leading

Remember the Power of Your Example   171
Practice Your Faith with Your Kids   175
Do Right Right   179
Do Wrong Right   183
Be a Personhood Leader   187

Conclusion   191
Summary of Tips   193
Notes   197
Acknowledgments   199

Foreword

Step into my office," I said to my husband one afternoon shortly after
we both arrived home from a long day. "My office" was the downstairs bathroom. A place where we could move out of earshot of the
kids, put our heads together, and determine how to move forward with
whatever parenting challenge we were facing. Some days we stepped
into the office, evaluated the situation, and knew the parenting tool that
was needed. Other days, we were stumped, not quite knowing what to
do as we stared at the situation in front of us.

As a contractor, my husband says that having the right tools can
greatly affect the ease or difficulty of a home repair project. While I
tend to accuse him of using that as an excuse to buy a new "toy" from
the home improvement store, I know he's absolutely right about the
difference the right tool can make. In the same way, having the right
"tools" as a parent can greatly affect the ease or difficulty of the parenting journey. When our parenting toolbox is full of the right parenting
tools, we're equipped to handle the diverse challenges our kids will in-
evitably throw our way.

As a mother of five, however, I know that even if you have the right
tool, there's nothing "simple" about parenting. What works for one kid,
often has absolutely no effect on another. Each child is unique and re-
sponds to life and leadership differently. Parenting requires us to seek
wisdom, be creative, and keep on learning.

Honestly, I always thought parenting was about what I would
teach my children. What I now know is that God used parenting to
mold and shape me. There's no doubt in my thirty years of parenting

experience, that I most definitely learned more in the process of parenting than I ever imparted to my children.

As a child psychologist, Todd Cartmell, fondly known as "Dr. Todd," also knows that parenting isn't so much about training the child as it is about training the parent. While his private practice is filled with helping kids navigate the challenges of life, he spends much of his time helping parents learn how to lead their kids well.

If you've never thought of yourself as a leader, think again. Parenting is really about leadership. The better equipped you are in leading your children, the better parent you'll be. The book you hold in your hands will give you the parenting power tools you need to lead well. Parenting isn't an easy formula with a guaranteed outcome. We can do our best and our kids can still make poor choices along the way. However, when we are well equipped for the job and are intentional about how we connect with our kids, we increase the probability that our kids will be great kids who make good choices.

I've personally benefitted from Todd's practical wisdom after attending many of his workshops at our Hearts at Home mom conferences. His sessions are always filled to capacity because our moms have come to trust his knowledge and experience. Dr. Todd's wisdom balanced with just the right amount of humor and illustrated with real-life examples makes this book an easy read. The short, quick-read chapters are perfect for a busy parent to read sitting in the carpool line or for couples to read aloud together each night before they head to bed.

Parenting isn't easy, but it's most definitely easier when you use the right tools for the job. A few pages a day and you're on your way to equipping yourself to be a great parent who raises great kids!

JILL SAVAGE

Hearts at Home Founder and CEO

INTRODUCTION

I once heard a story about a kindergarten teacher who, on the first day of school, asked a young boy what his name was.

"Johnny No-no," came the boy's reply.

The teacher looked puzzled. "Where did you get that name?" she asked.

"Well," explained Johnny, matter-of-factly. "Whenever my mom talks to me, she says, 'Johnny! No-no!'"

While it is possible that our little friend Johnny could have been a real handful, it would appear that his mother could have used a little help in responding to and guiding his challenging behavior.

In other words, she needed the right tools for the job.

This reminds me of a time a couple of months ago when I was attempting one of my semiannual handyman jobs around the house. We had just moved into a townhome, and all the smoke alarms needed replacing.

"Lora, have you seen the yellow utility knife anywhere?"

"Maybe it's in your toolbox."

"Nope, already looked."

"Then I don't know where it is."

Marital communication at its best.

In the process of replacing the alarms, I had discovered that there were a few wires to connect (red to red, black to black, and so on) and I needed to cut the colored plastic around a few of the wires so I could connect them more securely.

A utility knife was the right tool for the job.

However, it was nowhere to be found. So I tried to improvise. I knew we had a pair of scissors lying around somewhere, so I found those and attempted to cut the plastic by pressing the wire against one side of the scissors blade with my thumb and rotating it. Unfortunately, the blade was too dull and my thumb was too big and I soon realized that I was more likely to cut my thumb than the plastic.

So I quickly abandoned that idea and chose a smarter course of action. I hopped into the car and drove a couple of miles to a nearby Home Depot and purchased a new, bright yellow utility knife.

In other words, I got the right tool for the job.

The rest, as they say, was history.

Parenting is a lot like my experience with replacing the smoke alarms. You have a lot of jobs to do as a parent and your work never ends. You may even have a child like Johnny No-no. Depending on the particular job you are doing at the time, you will need many different tools. But you need the *right* tools if you want to get the job done properly.

As a child psychologist, I have had the privilege of working with kids and parents for over twenty years. I have seen tools that work and ones that don't. I have seen families that were built well and those that fell apart under the slightest pressure. In this book, I will show you eight simple tools to help you raise great kids and build a close and loving family that loves God and loves one another.

Here are the eight tools:

- Talking
- Listening
- Influencing

- Connecting
- Teaching
- Encouraging
- Correcting
- Leading

These tools are for both moms and dads, but it doesn't stop there. If you are a single parent, while you have your work cut out for you to be sure, you also can use each of these tools to help you teach and guide your kids as effectively as possible. But we are not done yet! Grandparents, aunts, uncles, and even nannies can use these tools to have a life-changing impact on the children in your life. In two-parent families, I have seen many families in which one parent connects while the other corrects. Bad idea. You *both* need to connect with your kids and you *both* need to be able to effectively correct them when needed. Each of these tools plays a critically important role in helping you raise great kids. Take a look at the list and choose a tool that you can do without.

There isn't one.

I know that while your family is a top priority, your schedule is already bursting at the seams with sports, school activities, household duties, work, and an endless list of things to do. The last thing you need is a long-winded parenting book to read (not to mention the guilt of never finishing it).

Already ahead of you on that one.

To make this book practical for busy parents, I have broken each of the eight tools into five brief chapters. No matter how busy you are, you *can* read a few pages at a time. Each chapter ends with a practical tip that will help you remember the main point of that chapter and a follow-up thought or action to consider that you can put into practice that very day.

The book of Proverbs tells us, "The simple believe anything, but the prudent give thought to their steps."[1] I'm sure you will agree that being a parent is one of the most important jobs God has given you. I know you love your kids and you want to be prudent about doing this job the very best you can.

Bottom line: If you are a parent who talks and listens to your kids, influences them with the power of your words, connects with them, teaches and encourages them, corrects them, and leads them through your example, then I believe you will change the trajectory of their lives. These are not tools to use for a while and then discard once your kids are eighteen. My boys are now both in their twenties and I need each of these tools as much as I did when they were three and five years old. These are tools you want to weave into the very nature of your parenting for as long as you are a parent.

That means forever.

It is my prayer that this book will help you do just that.

TOOL #1
TALKING

Chapter 1

Control Your
Volume Knob

D aniel was a ten-year-old boy who sat down on the overstuffed blue couch in my office one evening, with sad, tearful eyes.

"I don't like it when my dad yells at me," he said.

"What does he yell about?" I asked.

"If I did something wrong," he explained, "like if I leave the basement a mess."

"So, do you leave the basement a mess?"

"Yeah, sometimes I do."

"Okay, sometimes you leave the basement a mess and you know that your mom and dad are probably going to say something about it, right?" I ventured.

"Yeah, I know." Daniel continued, "But I just don't like the way he yells at me and gets so angry. It makes me not want to be around him."

Inwardly, I cringed. Those were just the words I didn't want to hear. Yet another parent/child relationship was starting to become damaged because of a parent's angry communication style.

Later, when I had a chance to meet his father, Randy, I discovered something I had suspected all along. Randy loved Daniel very much. He did not want to hurt their relationship; in fact, he very much wanted to build it.

In Randy's mind, he was doing his job as a dad. Daniel had been asked to clean up the basement many times and was not responding in a respectful way to this simple parental request.

No argument there.

The problem was the way Randy was doing his job as a dad. Daniel had a lesson to learn, no question about it. In fact, Randy, Becky (Daniel's mom), and Daniel all agreed that he should clean up any messes he made in the basement. And while the tidiness level of the basement was not a matter of national security, it was an issue that needed discussing.

However, without intending to, Randy's style of communication had become more like a sledgehammer that destroys rather than a gardening tool that nurtures. He wasn't setting out to damage his relationship with his son and somehow didn't even seem aware that this is what was happening. But that is exactly what his communication style was doing.

I have heard some fathers try to justify a strong-armed or intimidating discipline style by implying that their role as a father and leader gives them permission to use their emotions in this way with their children. Unfortunately for these fathers and their families, not only are they misunderstanding the basic fundamentals of leadership and effective communication, they are forgetting that Paul tells us to treat each other with patience, kindness, gentleness, and self-control.[1] And yes, that includes your family.

Luckily for Daniel, Randy made no such mistake. When Randy

realized the impact his communication style was having on his son, he started to cry, right in front of me.

That's right, he cried. Tears trickled down his cheeks as I told him how his son was becoming afraid to talk to him when he was angry. This was never the father Randy wanted to be, and yet this is the father he was becoming.

At Randy's request, we wasted no time getting to work on how he could repair things with his son. The first step was for him to apologize for his angry communication style. Yes, Daniel had not responded properly to the requests to clean up the basement; we were not overlooking that. But that was not the most important thing. The most important thing was that Randy had been damaging his relationship with the son he loved so much. He told Daniel he loved him and was sorry he had hurt their relationship with his yelling and that he would make every effort to speak to him in a respectful way, no matter what the topic was.

The second step was for Randy to follow up on that promise and turn down his volume knob. Which he did.

You should have seen Daniel's smile two weeks later. It was one for the record books.

The basement was clean too.

TALKING TIP #1:
Your communication style with your kids is REALLY, REALLY important. Not their communication style. Yours.

Consider:
How would you describe your communication style? What impact do you think your communication style has on your kids' communication style?

Chapter 2

If Unsure, Press Pause

My son Jake and I were recently watching a YouTube debate between two Oxford professors. The topic, a blend of science and philosophy (a favorite topic of ours), was whether recent advances in science have made belief in God no longer necessary. The debaters were John Lennox and Richard Dawkins, both professors and authors who are extremely intelligent and well respected in their fields. While holding markedly different viewpoints, both Lennox and Dawkins conducted their debate in a spirited, thought-provoking, and professional manner.

As we watched the debate unfold, something caught my eye. From time to time, Lennox would briefly pause in mid-sentence or between sentences and take a quick glance at his notes, obviously thinking of how he wanted to construct his thought, and then continue on with a well-crafted response or question for Dawkins.

He paused.

While Lennox's pauses were subtle, I recognized them because I have seen other experienced speakers use this technique as well. Whether listening to Hearts at Home founder Jill Savage deliver a keynote address to three thousand moms at a conference or to a pastor delivering a thought-provoking message to a modest Sunday-morning congregation, a brief pause communicates a positive message from the speaker to the listener:

> I am in control of what I am saying.
> I am not letting a momentary rush of adrenaline take over.
> I am going to choose my words carefully, because what I am saying is important.

On the other hand, I have had many moms and dads tell me that in moments of frustration they have blurted out hurtful words and made angry comments to their kids that they wish they could take back.

> Stupid
> Lazy
> You do *nothing around here.*
> Loser
> Worthless
> You are always getting in trouble.

But they can't. Instead, those hurtful words or comments will echo around in their kids' memory. Words that were not meant. Words that do not reflect how Mom or Dad really feel. Words that were simply heated by an angry moment and escaped in a blast of frustration.

Words that could have been prevented.

With a pause.

I have realized there are a few things we, as parents, can learn from seasoned communicators like John Lennox. After all, we are communicators too. In fact, we are having some of the most important discussions of our lives, every day—with our kids.

Sometimes, the emotional rush of a frustrated moment puts us at risk for saying things we don't mean and will only regret. The Bible tells us, "The words of the reckless pierce like swords, but the tongue of the wise brings healing."[2] It is at these moments of frustration we need to do exactly what an expert communicator would do.

Pause.

A pause may take only a second or two, but it gives your brain enough time to do a quick reboot while you ask yourself a few key questions or give yourself a few timely reminders:

What do I really want to say?

What is the best way to say it?

If I want my kids to talk respectfully when they are mad, then I must do the same.

I want my child to copy my communication style, not me copy theirs.

These refocusing thoughts can make the difference between a discussion that ends well and one that ends worse than before you started.

We've all had a few of those.

If you would like to avoid this type of hurtful, unproductive discussion in the future, you need to remember one thing: to pause.

TALKING TIP #2:
If you are not sure what to say, a brief pause
can make all the difference between wise words and hurtful ones.

Consider:

What are a few situations when pausing will help you be a more effective communicator with your kids? Why do you think pausing makes a difference?

Chapter 3

Start with You

I t is a chilly September Saturday afternoon and fourteen-year-old Colton and his dad are watching a college football game on TV. Mom is catching up on some work, content to see her son and husband spending some quality time together.

Perfect.

Ten-year-old Luci and her mom take their weekly trip to Luci's dance lesson. Luci listens to her iPod in the car and is excited to see her friends at the dance studio. Mom chats with her own dance mom friends during the lesson and leafs through an article from her new magazine. On the way home, Luci fills her mom in on a bit of relationship drama she learned from her dance friends and then settles back in with her iPod for the rest of the trip.

Perfect again.

Or maybe not.

Watching a favorite television show together. Taking your child to a music lesson or sports practice. Having dinner at your favorite pizza restaurant. Putting a puzzle together on a snowy winter day. These positive situations happen hundreds of times in most families in the course of daily life. But as described above, they are not necessarily transforming. While spending time together is great, it is only one part of the recipe. Just like chocolate chip cookies would be cruelly incomplete without the chocolate chips, we desperately need the second key ingredient.

That ingredient is you. Not your physical body—we already have that. Your kids need you. Your presence, your interest, your engagement. Your kids need to unmistakably know that you are more interested in them than in your magazine, the football game, or whatever the activity may be.

That's transforming.

And it starts with you.

How do you do this? It is not as difficult as you may think.

Engage first. This simply means that when doing an activity with your kids, you start talking before they do. When you engage first, you are showing your kids you are interested in *them*. You may like football, but you are really interested in them. You may enjoy playing a board game together, but it is their life you are really interested in. The key is in the fact that you engage *first*. This shows intention; you are not just responding to their comments—you are the one kicking off the conversation in the first place.

Ask questions about their opinions, thoughts, feelings, and current activities. *When I engage, what am I supposed to say?* Engaging questions can include just about anything as long as it is about your kids. If you were really into vintage hot rods and were at a classic car show with some unbelievable cars to look at, you wouldn't have much trouble thinking of questions to ask the car owners about how they restored their classic hot rods.

In the same way, when you think about your kids and the current details of their lives, it won't be difficult to come up with lots of things to ask them about. Here's a starter list:

Things that have happened, or might happen, that day
Friendships
School
Current activities/sports
Favorite things to do
Things they would like to do someday
Anything that is challenging for them right now

Pick a topic and begin. As often as possible, make your questions of the open-ended variety (e.g., "What was something fun that you did today?") so you avoid ending up with a bunch of single-word responses. Your question may immediately lead to a meaningful discussion or you may hop around to a few different topics. Every conversation is different. Sometimes there is something going on and sometimes there isn't. But every time, your kids will know that you showed interest in them.

Warm body language (smile, eye contact, physical touch). If you really want your time to be connecting, make sure it comes fully loaded with plenty of warm nonverbal body language. It is well known that people actually pay more attention to your nonverbal communication than to the actual words you say. So put a little science savvy to work and season your conversation with warm body language, such as little touches, squeezes, and smiles.

The next time Colton and his dad watched a football game, Colton's dad used commercials and halftime to ask his son about sports/activities he might like to try someday. On Luci's next trip to dance class, her mom took advantage of the car time to ask Luci about her clos-est friends and how she handles the drama that can happen with fifth-grade girls. Luci didn't even turn her iPod on.

Same activities, lots more connection.

It starts with you.

TALKING TIP #3:
When you initiate conversations with your kids, it shows them that at that moment, you are more interested in them than in anything else.

Consider:
How does it make your kids feel when you initiate a conversation with them? How do you feel when someone shows interest in your life?

Chapter 4

Be Easy to Listen To

Have you ever wondered what it is like to listen to you?
That is kind of a scary question.

Gabriel was a young boy sitting in my office who, in typical nine-year-old fashion, told his mother what it is like for him when she corrects him.

Gabriel: "My mom is always yelling at me."

Mom: "I don't yell at him. Well, maybe occasionally I do. But if he listened better, there would be no yelling at all."

While Gabriel may have been guilty of some exaggeration in his use of the word "always" (i.e., I'm sure his mother doesn't always yell at him), his mother's response indicates that she was not interested in really hearing about what it feels like to be on the other end of one of her reprimands. In fact, you may have noticed how quickly she admitted yelling but then actually blamed it on Gabriel, who, by the way, is not responsible for Mom's choice to yell.

However, I cannot be too hard on this mother, as I have found myself in the same place on occasion. When I have asked myself this question—What is it like to listen to me?—almost immediately I realize I'm hesitant to learn the answer. Why? Because, truth be told, I like to think that when I talk to my kids, flowers burst into bloom, rainbows adorn the sky, and high in the heavens above, angels are belting out the "Hallelujah Chorus."

I don't really want to own up to the fact that I may:

Drone on and on
Be too critical
Overlook my kids' positive choices, or
Express my frustration in a counterproductive way

But I know that sometimes I do.

I always find it rather ironic when a difficult-to-listen-to parent complains their kids don't want to listen to them. I am guessing that if I were their child, I wouldn't want to listen to them either.

QUESTION: *Who wants to listen to someone who is hard to listen to?*

Answer: No one.

I have seen plenty of strong parent-child relationships, and I have seen my share of damaged ones. The strongest relationships all have one thing in common: The kids feel comfortable talking (and listening) to their parents. If you really want your kids to be able to talk with you about anything, then I have a suggestion for you: become an easy-to-listen-to parent.

"When should I be easy to listen to?" you may ask. My answer: Anytime you are saying anything you want your kids to be open to.

That means pretty much all the time.

During the easy topics and during the difficult topics.

Especially during the difficult topics.

It is during the difficult topics we tend to become less easy to listen to. Our volume level rises. Our tone becomes more intense. Before you know it, you are talking to your kids the way you would never want anyone to talk to you. Your communication style begins to shut down your kids instead of open them up. It pushes them away instead of drawing them near.

If you want your kids to want to listen to you, then take inventory of a few things:

Your volume
Your tone
Your choice of words
Your respectfulness
Your self-control

Notice the first three letters in each of the above items: Y O U. Every word you say only leaves your mouth with your permission. You don't control your kids' responses, but you do control your words, volume level, and tone. As you read through the above list, what areas stand out as ways you need to improve? Can you imagine what your family life will be like if you make those improvements?

Remember a recent conversation with your kids that went awry and imagine how that conversation might have been different if you had made different choices with your words, tone, and volume. If you had paused when you needed to. Imagine the conversation ending with a hug and a smile instead of with hurtful words, angry silence, and a damaged relationship.

This is the kind of communication your family needs.

This is the kind of communication God calls us to.

Your kids won't do this naturally; they need to learn it from you. You won't do it perfectly and neither will I. But we need to get started, and one great place to start is with the simple question: "Would I like to listen to me?"

TALKING TIP #4:
When you are an easy-to-listen-to parent,
your kids will be more open to the important
lessons you want to teach.

Consider:
If you are honest, would you consider yourself more of an easy-to-listen-to parent or a hard-to-listen-to parent? What is one thing you can change to make yourself easier to listen to?

Chapter 5

Play a Game of Catch

I remember playing soccer with a group of friends at lunch one day back at J. P. Dallas Elementary School. I grew up in a small, coastal town in British Columbia, where we were often aware of the unmistakable (and not very pleasant) smell of the local paper mill. As you might guess, the sport of choice for me and my friends was hockey, but since we couldn't play hockey at school and nobody had really ever heard of football, soccer was the next best thing.

This particular day, as we were playing soccer on the large grassy field, one of the boys inexplicably took off with the soccer ball and started playing with some other kids on the far side of the field. There we stood, looking on in amazement, as our soccer game had just been hijacked.

You can't play soccer without a ball.

I have seen the same thing happen in family discussions. The discussion is moving along nicely and then, out of the blue, it gets hijacked. The hijacker is usually a parent who takes it upon themselves to deliver either an angry-toned or long discourse meant to teach, reprimand, vent, or simply bore their kids into compliance.

I saw this happen with nine-year-old Cassie. She and her parents were sitting in my office one evening as we were discussing Cassie's behavior. The discussion was moving along well until Theresa, her mother, felt the need to speak at length about Cassie's rude behaviors, dating from about six months before. For good measure, she threw in key words like "always" and "never" (e.g., "She *always* argues about everything," and "She *never* says thank you") and made negative character references by using words like ungrateful and selfish.

Just before I decided to stop this counterproductive onslaught, I glanced at Cassie. She had slouched back in her chair, given off an exasperated sigh, and was staring at the corner of my office where the ceiling met the wall. This told me that her mother had pulled this move before.

Probably many times.

At that point, a funny thing had already happened. Even though Theresa was still talking, a conversation was no longer taking place. Quicker than you can say *The Tonight Show with Jimmy Fallon*, the dialogue had turned into a monologue. It is like two people playing a game of catch with a softball and then, all of a sudden, one person simply decides to hold on to the ball. The game of catch has ended. The player without the ball stands around waiting, not sure if she will get a chance to have the ball again or not.

A healthy family discussion can be likened to a simple game of catch. The ball represents what is being said. The first person tosses the ball and the second person focuses on catching it. Then the roles reverse, with the second person tossing the ball, gently of course, so the first person can catch it. Back and forth, back and forth, like a friendly game of catch.

The two most common mistakes that I have seen parents make

when talking to their kids are holding on to the ball too long and throwing it back too hard.

Both these mistakes are conversation killers. No one likes it when one person hogs the ball or when someone whips a 90 mph fastball at them. If you want to have productive conversations with your kids, remember to:

Keep your comments brief. This is the best way to keep your kids active and involved in a conversation. Intentionally make your comments short and to the point. This is like a game of catch where no one holds the ball for too long. It keeps your kids involved and responding and communicates that you are interested in what they have to say.

Make your comments easy to catch (or listen to). Just like your momma told you, be thoughtful about what you say and how you say it. For example, if you have to discuss a negative behavior, do so in the way that you would like it discussed with you, if the tables were turned.

Describe a positive behavior (yes, there are some).

Briefly describe the negative behavior and how it makes things difficult for your child and for others (e.g., creates conflict, brings negative consequences).

Talk together with your child to come up with a plan for how to handle the situation better in the future.

Remember, there are many lessons God wants you to teach your kids. You will find hundreds of teachable moments that can make a profound impact in their lives. However, those moments will only be teachable if your kids are open to what you have to say. Your goal is to always talk in a way that opens your kids up, not in a way that shuts them down.

In other words, give them a chance to hold the ball and toss them balls they can catch.

TALKING TIP #5:
**When your conversations are like a
friendly game of catch, everyone will want to be involved.**

Consider:
How do you think it will impact your family discussions and relationships if you keep your comments brief and talk to your kids the way you would like someone to talk to you?

TOOL #2
LISTENING

Chapter 6

Listen First

I recently saw a YouTube clip from an Austin Powers movie. Dr. Evil has a somewhat dysfunctional relationship with almost everybody. Including his son. I guess that is to be expected with a name like Dr. Evil.

On this occasion, Dr. Evil was sitting at his conference table with all of his top people, plotting his next step in taking over the world. Also at the table was his son Scott, who had a sensible contribution to make to the discussion. However, Dr. Evil was not interested in hearing it. It went something like this:

Dr. Evil: "Scott, you just don't get it, do you? You don't."
Scott: "It's no—"
Dr. Evil: "Shhh!"
Scott: "But—"
Dr. Evil: "Shhh!"
Scott: "All—"
Dr. Evil: "Shhh!"
Scott: "All I'm saying—"

Dr. Evil: "Shhh!"
Scott: "They're going to get away—"
Dr. Evil: "Shhh!"
Scott: "I—"
Dr. Evil: "Shhh!"
Scott: "Would—"
Dr. Evil: "Knock, knock."
Scott: "Who's there?"
Dr. Evil: "Shhh!"

And on it went.

The reason this scene tickled so many funny bones is that it humorously illustrated a frustrating experience we have all encountered: wanting to say something but not being given the chance. We all want to be the first to talk. We all want to state our point of view and persuade others that we are right.

In a family situation, this fight for who gets the microphone first is usually settled by power or authority. The parent who has the more intimidating voice and who controls the privileges usually wins. The sibling who is the oldest, strongest, or loudest often wins.

Or do they?

In my experience, it is actually the opposite.

The Bible tells us, "To answer before listening—that is folly and shame."[1] I remember learning the truth of that verse one afternoon when my wife, Lora, and I were having a bit of an argument. Normally, we would proceed in a typically reasonable manner, with each of us sharing our opinions back and forth. But this time, I decided to do something different.

I decided to listen before talking.

"You go first," I said.

Those three words have had a profound impact on my communication style to this very day. Lora began to explain her point of view and I did not interrupt. I sincerely tried to put my own viewpoint aside for a moment and look at things from her perspective.

What happened next was totally unexpected. As I listened first, I found my point of view beginning to soften. She didn't seem as unreasonable as she had just seconds before. It was all making more sense now.

Amazing.

Lora finished talking and I repeated what I believed were her main points to make sure I had listened correctly. I had. Now it was my turn to talk and I remembered exactly what I was going to say.

Except now I didn't want to say it.

I responded in an entirely different way than if I had spoken first. I remember feeling quite glad I had listened first. It almost felt like I had an unfair advantage. What I said next was so much better, calmer, and more mature than what I had planned to say. The conversation ended on a positive note.

I believe it was because I listened first.

I have experienced the same thing with my boys many times. I personally consider listening first to be my secret weapon. In any conversation, it gives me a chance to get more information about how another person feels and thinks about a topic before I respond. After all, what is there to lose? I can always say what I want. But what I wanted to say just might get a makeover that will turn out even better when it's my turn to speak.

Try listening first with your kids today. You may be surprised at how wise and self-controlled you sound. Your kids might be surprised too.

I can honestly tell you that there are more than a few times I have regretted talking first. But I have never regretted listening first.

LISTENING TIP #1:
Listening first will always help you
respond more wisely than if you had talked first.

Consider:
Do you tend to talk first or listen first? How will listening first help you as a parent? As a spouse?

Chapter 7

Listen to Understand

Can you guess what this is?

CLUE #1: You can hear it rattling along beside you down the road, filled with all sorts of loose material that needs to be transferred from one place to another.

CLUE #2: It is a favorite Tonka toy of little boys (and possibly girls).

Answer: A dump truck.

I would like you to do something you have probably never done before. Picture your kids as if they were dump trucks.

Because, in a way, they are.

Dump trucks have a lot of cubic space inside of them. So do your kids. The only difference is that while dump trucks get filled up with dirt and gravel, your kids get filled up with something much different—thoughts, feelings, opinions, hopes, dreams, and much more.

Excitement about making the basketball team.
Disappointment about doing poorly on a social studies test.

Hurt feelings because of how a friend treated them on the
playground.

Concern for abused animals.

Worry about what sixth grade will be like.

All of these things are important to you, because your kids are important to you. Your kids are like dump trucks that are filled with valuable cargo, like one filled with diamonds.

This brings us to another feature common to all dump trucks: Sooner or later, they get filled up. They can only handle so much cargo. And once they get filled up, there is only one thing for them to do.

Unload.

Listening is simply letting your kids unload their truck. Because that truck is going to get filled up again, and your child is going to learn where the best places are for unloading hers. In other words, she will figure out who really takes the time to listen to her. The best listeners she finds will be the people she will unload her truck with over and over again.

You want to be one of her favorite unloading zones.

If you listen to understand, you will.

Listening to understand simply means that you are remembering that everything in your child's truck is of great value to you (remember, it is full of diamonds). Because of this, you *really* want to make sure that you catch *every* diamond pouring out of that truck. It is really just following Jesus' words when He told us, "Do to others as you would have them do to you."[2] You like it when someone listens to understand how you really think and feel because it makes you feel valuable and important.

Your kids will feel that way too.

How do you listen to understand?

Follow these steps:

Don't add new information, just listen. Remember, she is unloading her truck. It doesn't help for you to be shoveling in new information while she is trying to unload. You can share new thoughts and ideas later, once her truck is empty. But when she is talking, just listen.

Ask clarifying questions. Questions that help you better understand her thoughts, feelings, and perspectives are great, because they communicate that you are really trying to understand her. They might sound like this:

Help me understand why you felt that way.

What made you think he did that on purpose?

How did you feel when that happened?

Use reflective statements. Another great way to show that you are listening to understand is to make reflective statements. A reflective statement is just a short summary of what you think your child's main thoughts or feelings are. It is just a way to double-check and make sure that you really understand what she is trying to say.

"Let's see if I have this right. You're really hurt about what Lisa said and you're confused about why she would say something like that."

"Okay. So, you're saying that you think that the consequence of losing Xbox for one week was unfair; you think it should have been less time."

"You sound really excited about this sleepover coming up!"

When you do your best to sincerely try to understand everything your kids are unloading from their truck, they will feel valued and important. When you listen first *and* listen to understand, your conversations will get off on the right foot. Better yet, your kids will learn that you are an easy parent to talk with. So when difficult situations come along (which they will), your kids will already know that one of the most safe and encouraging places to unload their truck is waiting for them at home.

That place is called Mom and Dad.

LISTENING TIP #2:
When you listen to understand, your kids will want to unload their trucks in your zone on a regular basis.

Consider:
What do you think of the dump truck analogy? Why is allowing your kids to empty their trucks so important? When you listen to understand, what does that communicate to your kids?

Chapter 8

Listen Often

Nora was a twelve-year-old girl who was having trouble with some kids at school and was feeling confused and depressed. As we talked about what was going on and ways she could handle things, I asked her if she had talked to her parents about the situation.

"No."

"Do you talk with them much about things?" I asked.

"Not really."

"Well, what is going on at school is pretty big. Do you think it might be a good idea to tell your parents about it?" I pressed.

"Nah, it would feel too weird," she explained.

"What do you mean, weird?" I asked.

"I'm just not used to talking to them about stuff."

There it is.

This young girl was more comfortable talking about some of the important issues in her life with an adult she had known for less than a month (yours truly) than with the two adults who loved her more than anything on this earth.

That's not quite how it should be.

Have you ever been walking on a paved nature trail and then noticed, off to one side, a path that had been made, not intentionally, but simply as the result of people treading over it often? Because that path has been traveled on frequently it has now become easy to walk along.

However, if that path were abandoned, what would happen to it? The natural growth of foliage would gradually overtake it until one day it would no longer be recognizable as a path. The lack of use would make it difficult to navigate.

Nora's relationship with her parents had become like the path overgrown with foliage. Perhaps it had never been really cleared off in the first place. Either way, the lack of ordinary talk about life's joys and challenges had made the communication pathway between Nora and her parents feel like an unfamiliar route she was not comfortable traveling along when she had an extra-heavy load to carry.

How do you prevent this happening with your kids, or if your communication pathway has already become overgrown with foliage because of a lack of use, how do you clear the pathway so that it is once again easy to move on?

You listen, and you listen often.

We have talked about listening first and listening to understand. But those do you no good if used once a year. A pathway in the woods emerges because it has been trodden upon frequently. If you want your kids to be comfortable talking with you, then you will need to offer them plenty of possibilities.

Here's how you do it:

Look for opportunities. You never know when the chance for a meaningful discussion will present itself, so be on the lookout. After school, during a dinner conversation, during a car ride, while shopping, while playing a game or sporting activity—any of these situations could provide an opportunity for you to talk with your kids about things that are important to them.

Create opportunities. While you are waiting for opportunities to present themselves, you can make a few of your own. One of the best ways I know to do this is to get into the habit of a regular check-in. When our boys were younger, Lora made it a habit to check in with them right after school. When she ran into the typical one-word responses—"How was school today?" "Fine." "What did you learn today?" "Nothing."—she changed her style by asking simple detailed questions: "Who did you sit beside at lunch today?" and "What is one thing you did at recess?" Sticking with this conversation method produced many great occasions for talking about what was happening in our boys' lives.

Since I wasn't home when they returned from school, I did a regular check-in with them before bedtime. Before we would say our nightly prayers, I would ask them how things were going and if there was anything they wanted to talk over or pray about. Sometimes there was and sometimes there wasn't. But every night, they knew I had expressed interest in what was happening in their lives.

Over the years, we had many good after-school and bedtime conversations. Keep in mind that those conversations happened because Lora and I chose to check in with them. And every conversation was like another walk down the path, with our boys becoming more and more comfortable talking to Lora and me about whatever was on their mind.

If you want your kids to come to you when something important is happening in their life, or when they need some guidance, make sure the path to your doorstep is already well worn from frequent travel.

LISTENING TIP #3:
If you want your kids to be comfortable
talking to you, make sure they get plenty of
opportunity to practice.

Consider:

What are some ways you can listen to your kids on a regular basis?
When are the best times for check-ins with your kids?

Chapter 9

Listen to Everything

Mom, check out this video on YouTube!
How come I can't have a Facebook account?
Dad, why did you and Mom get divorced?
Whoa, that was so awesome!
I'll never make the basketball team.
I really want a pet. Can we get one?
Why can't we get that video game? All my friends have it.

The stream of comments, questions, and exclamations is endless. Hundreds of different thoughts and feelings from ecstatic to exasperated, from delighted to disillusioned. They may come at convenient times or when you are in the middle of an important phone call. They may come early in the morning or in the middle of the night.

But come they will. From the time your kids learn to talk until the day they move out (and even after), there will be thousands of communication opportunities, especially if you have been creating them and making a well-worn communication pathway as we discussed in the last chapter. Of course, if you are the parent of college-aged children (or older), you know that opportunities for communication don't stop when your kids move out. They may become less frequent, but they continue to happen and always have the potential to be meaningful.

Recent discussions in our home with our boys, both now in their early twenties, have included the following topics:

A recent marriage engagement
College plans
Saving money
Food for the wedding reception
A recent podcast by a favorite pastor
A slow night at work
Filing income taxes
How to fix an iPod
Opinions about a recent movie
Training our new puppy
A television series we enjoy

While the topics have ranged from lighthearted to life changing, a thread ties each one together. Every one of them is important. Every one of them leaves our boys feeling either more connected with us or less. Every one of them gives Lora and me a chance to build our relationship closer and to show that we care about them and what they think.

The little things and the big things. It is our job to listen to both.

Last night, Lora and I were watching a show on Netflix when Luke walked in from work. As usual, we instinctively paused the show and spent several minutes listening to him describe his evening's experiences as a server at a local restaurant. We were in no hurry to get back to our program; connecting with him was far more important. Now, I am not expecting a Parent of the Year medal for simply pausing a television show, but I have no doubt that because we did, Luke felt valued and listened to.

It is easy to think that the little things are unimportant while the big things are momentous. This is a mistake. Remember the dump truck? It is filled with diamonds. Some may be smaller and some bigger, but they are all diamonds.

That is the thing to remember.

Of course, you may not be able to listen to everything exactly when your kids want you to. Your kids need to learn that they are not the center of the universe. Other people have needs and obligations and sometimes your kids will have to wait. That is an important lesson of life we all must learn. But even when your kids have to wait, it is important that you follow up with them.

Waiting is one thing; being forgotten is another.

In addition to the everyday discussions Lora and I try to always be attentive to, one fun way we talked about a lot of different topics was to use a book of questions, the kind you can pick up at any bookstore.[3] These are great for mealtimes, car rides, family times, or any time you have a few minutes to talk and no pressing agenda. In fact, we often just left a book like this in our minivan and took turns picking a number (one of our books had 1001 questions) and then we would take turns giving responses. Some questions resulted in short fun answers while others led to longer discussions of opinions, memories, current world events, and spiritual issues.

Little things and big things.

Every conversation is a chance to show your kids you are interested in what they are feeling and how they are thinking.

Every one builds your relationship.

Every one is a diamond.

LISTENING TIP #4:
When you remember that everything your kids share with you is a diamond, you will want to listen to every single word.

Consider:
How does viewing all of your kids' thoughts and feelings as diamonds impact your desire to listen to and connect with them?

Chapter 10

Listen with
Your Entire Body

W hen I was studying music back in the '80s in junior college, I remember being introduced to "Doctor, doctor" jokes by one of my jazz band instructors. I'm not sure why I hadn't heard them before; perhaps they just never made it up to my part of Canada.

One of my favorites applies to the topic of listening:

Woman: "Doctor, doctor, my husband never listens to me."

Doctor: "Next."

In order to understand why being a good listener is so important, we must first understand the purpose of talking. Put in the simplest of terms, when your kids talk to you, they are taking their thoughts or feelings and sharing them with another person. This is no little thing. They may be sharing basic information (such as the amount of milk left in the fridge), or something far more personal (such as an opinion about school rules or feelings about a friend). Either way, they are literally taking something personal from inside their brain where it was private and are choosing to share it with you.

A little melodramatic?

I don't think so.

When your kids talk, they are giving you a glimpse into who they are. They may not think about it quite this way at the moment, but they are sharing a bit of themselves with you.

They are taking a risk.

Maybe you will listen.

Maybe you won't.

Maybe you will really care about what they say.

Maybe you will brush it off because you are watching TV at the moment.

Listening is your response to your kids' vulnerability. When your kids talk to you, listening says, "You are *valuable* to me." That is why it is such a powerful thing. They are sharing something from inside themselves and they want to know that it is important to you. Because that means *they* are important to you. You are not just anyone to your kids. You are their mom or dad, the one they want to be able to talk to about anything. The one they *need* to talk with about many things. Your kids want to feel safe with you, so they do not have to fear being criticized or feeling stupid when they share their feelings, state their opinions, or make a mistake.

Listening matters.

One day I was talking with Natalie, a second grader, and her mother in my office. As we were discussing Natalie's behavior, her mother noticed that she was starting to squirm around and look anywhere but at me.

"Natalie, listen with your *entire* body," she said.

Immediately, Natalie sat up straight and looked right at me. She obviously knew what Mom was getting at.

We could all learn a lesson about listening from Natalie.

Listen with your entire body.

Have you ever been talking to someone and gotten the feeling that they weren't really interested in what you were saying? How did you come to that conclusion? My guess is that their words did not tell you.

Their body did.

Body language is a key part of being a good listener. Let's do a head-to-toe inventory.

Your eyes. When your kids are talking to you, do you look away from your work, your book, or the television, and look directly at them? Your kids know that where your eyes are looking is where your attention is.

Your ears. If you have learned to listen first, then your ears will take priority over your mouth. As a result, the words you speak will be that much more helpful and encouraging.

Your mouth. If you are listening to understand, your mouth will not be adding new information into the truck just yet, but will first be asking clarifying questions and making reflective statements to make sure that you have caught every diamond your child is sending your way.

Your neck to knees. When your kids talk to you, do you turn your entire body to face them? Is your stance open? Are your arms uncrossed? Are your hands still? Does everything about your body communicate your number one goal at that moment—to listen? Why? Because everything in their truck is valuable to you.

Your feet. Do you make it a point to find listening opportunities and to do regular check-ins with your kids? Do you ask them about the little things and the big things?

Listening with your entire body is a good way to remember all of the listening points we have covered in this section. There is no substitute for being a good listener. You simply can't have a close relationship without being one.

Think about that.

Being a good listener is a must if you want a close relationship with your kids. A close relationship is a must for you to have the influence on your kids God wants you to have. And just like my little second grade friend, it starts with listening with your entire body.

LISTENING TIP #5:
When you listen with your entire body, it shows your kids
that their thoughts and feelings are VALUABLE to you,
which means that THEY are valuable to you.

Consider:
Can you tell when someone is really listening to you? How do you feel when you are really listened to? How will listening with your entire body impact your relationship with your kids?

TOOL #3
INFLUENCING

Chapter 11

Remember Who
They Are

I f you saw the Disney movie *Tangled*, you know that Rapunzel (who was a princess, of course) was held captive in a tower by a woman who had kidnapped her as an infant and was now pretending to be her mother. After an unauthorized escapade away from the tower, Rapunzel had just been told by her so-called mother that the boy she liked had betrayed her (spoiler alert—he hadn't) and she would never be allowed to leave the tower again. Heartbroken and utterly disillusioned, Rapunzel lay on her bed with her color-challenged chameleon trying to console her. As she gazed up at her ceiling, filled with murals she had painted as a child, Rapunzel recognized a picture of a certain star she had unintentionally woven into her many paintings. She then realized that this was the star that represented the royal family—she was the lost princess!

In a flash, she remembered who she was.

That changed everything.

Many of us can benefit from the same kind of lightbulb moment when it comes to our kids. We need to remember who they really are. Strange as it may seem, it is easy to forget. With diapers to change, electrical cords to grab out of their hands, soccer games to drive to, tantrums to quell, sibling arguments to stop, homework to help with, meals to prepare, teeth and showers to make sure are brushed and taken, and bedtime routines to get through, it is easy to lose sight of who your kids are.

Here is a new way to think about your kids. Think of them as cereal boxes. That's right, cereal boxes. Not just any kind of cereal box, but the best kind—the kind with the special prize hidden inside. God, of course, is the manufacturer, like Nabisco or General Mills. And He has made a cereal box (perhaps a few of them) just for you. Better yet, He has filled those cereal boxes, not just with one prize, but with many special gifts, talents, and characteristics that will only be discovered with time.

As a parent, it is your job to help your kids find out what special "prizes" God has put inside. One type of prize may come in the form of a special *personality trait*. Your child may have a built-in tendency to be funny, caring, witty, insightful, teachable, loyal, responsible, hardworking, or easygoing. Another type of prize may be a special *ability or area of strength* that your child has. For instance, he or she may be naturally gifted in reading, soccer, conversations, a musical instrument, writing, drama, swimming, art, singing, or electronics, to name a few possibilities. A third type of prize may be a special *passion or interest* your child develops, such as a love for animals, a heart for the needy, or a fascination with flight.

So, how do you help your kids find the prizes that God has placed in their box? Try these ideas on for size:

Be on the lookout. We already know that God has placed prizes in your kids; now it's a matter of your noticing them. So be alert. When you observe that your child is good at telling jokes, often shows kindness to others, seems naturally talented at a certain activity, or shows a strong interest in a specific area, take notice—you may be witnessing one of the prizes God has placed inside of them.

Point out their positive strengths and traits. When you see a potential prize emerge, point it out in an encouraging way. It may sound like this:

"Julie, I have noticed that you are very good at explaining things."

"Paul, you have a real knack for telling good jokes."

"Megan, I have noticed that you are a good friend to others. You are loyal and always try to see the best in people. No wonder people want to be friends with you."

"Jayden, you seem to really like animals. We should get a book on your favorite kind of animal and read it together."

"Susie, you are one of the hardest workers I have ever seen. Even when something is hard or boring, you really stick with it. That's quite impressive. Good job!"

Engage in the activity with them (when possible). Depending on the trait, ability, or area of passion that you see developing in your child, you have a wonderful chance to connect with your child by engaging in that activity with them. When my boys got involved in karate, I started taking lessons too. As a result, I was able to participate with them and knowledgably encourage them and help with their practices and tournament preparation. Because of this, we enjoyed many fun classes, home practices, and tournaments together.

You may research a topic together, engage in serving opportunities, read through a joke book together, go to band concerts, or be the ever-encouraging audience for your burgeoning young magician as he asks you to "pick a card" for the thousandth time. Whatever the area is, your regular participation and unflagging encouragement will help that "prize" flourish into all that God wants it to become.

What prizes are inside the cereal boxes that God has given you?

INFLUENCING TIP #1:
When you remember who your kids really are,
you can help them discover the gifts God has placed inside them.

Consider:
How does it help you to think of your kids as cereal boxes? What are some of the traits, abilities, or areas of interest you see developing in each of your kids? How can you encourage your child in that area?

Chapter 12

Understand the Power of Your Words

Kevin was a nine-year-old boy with tears starting to well up in his eyes. "I hate school," he said, looking down at the floor. As we talked, it turned out it was not his teacher or the schoolwork that was the problem. A few kids had begun teasing him and calling him names.

As we talked about how to respond in these teasing moments, it became apparent that the actual words that had been said to him had begun to leave a mark on him. "No one likes me, they all think I'm dumb," Kevin claimed, looking thoroughly dejected. Not only did we have to work on how he responded to teasing, we now had to correct his view of himself.

This brought to mind a teenaged girl named Olivia I had seen a few years earlier. Because of the careless comments of a few thoughtless boys, she had come to the conclusion that she was unattractive. It took a lot of work to undo the damage a few unkind words had done.

In case you haven't already noticed: Words have a lot of power.

But I am guessing you already know that.

The Bible tells us, "The tongue has the power of life and death. . . ."[1] Truer words have never been written. This concept applies to us as parents as well. Your words have tremendous power to your kids. There are two reasons for this. The first is simple: You are their mom or dad. From the very beginning, you are the ones who changed their diapers, fed them, saw them take their first steps, took them to school, watched them on play dates, and kept them safe. They have learned to trust in you and what you say.

Of course, they don't think that you are absolutely infallible or incapable of making a mistake. If they do think that, it will simply be a matter of time before that bubble is burst. However, what you say about *them* has a special significance. Why? Because you see them at their best and at their worst. You *know* them better than any other adult on this planet. They *know* that you *know* them. Therefore, they tend to believe that what you say about them may actually be true.

The second reason that your words are powerful is that they impact how your kids think. The way your kids think is the rudder that directs not only how they feel but the choices they make. The choices they make over time will shape the course of their life and define their future.

I'd say that's powerful.

For better or worse, your words shape your kids from the inside out.

For example, take the girl who is regularly affirmed by her parents and reminded of how much they love her and are proud of her. Even when she makes a poor choice, her parents help turn it into a productive lesson that can help her make a better choice next time. She will start to see herself as God's handiwork[2] and develop a healthy understanding of who she is (with both her strengths and faults), holding a positive outlook toward her future.

In contrast, consider the boy who often hears critical words from his parents but few positive ones. He begins to believe that nothing he does will be good enough, which leads to feelings of rejection and distance. He starts to spend more time in his room. Maybe he will work harder to try to earn his parents' approval. Or maybe he will just give up and look elsewhere for acceptance, even in the wrong places. Maybe he will hide away in the world of video games and faceless online friends. He is filled with incorrect beliefs about who he is, which shape his decisions and will likely lead his future in the wrong direction.

How do you use the power of your words to influence your kids?

Remember that every word counts. Every time you talk to your kids, remember that your words are shaping the way they think about themselves. You want your kids to think about themselves accurately. You want them to know that they are God's handiwork, that they sometimes make mistakes and bad choices like any of us, and that God can shape them into something wonderful. Make it a goal to look for opportunities to remind your kids of who God says they are.

Speak to your kids the way you would like to be spoken to. I have always found Jesus' words for us to treat others as we would like to be treated[3] to be a perfect verse for parents and children alike to remember. How would you like someone to talk to you after a basketball game, or about a report card? Talk to your kids that same way.

Capture your child's potential. Your words show your kids who you think they are. Let them hear that you know they are full of great stuff—not perfect of course, but packed with loads of potential put there by God Himself.

Avoid damaging words. Make it a goal not to let any damaging words cross your lips. Stay away from hurtful words that simply express your own frustration or lack of emotional control at the moment. This is when you need to pause, as we discussed, or postpone your discussion for a later time, rather than say something that will influence your child's thinking and self-view in a negative and inaccurate way.

Your words *will* have a lasting impact on your kids. As the writer of Proverbs 18:21 reminded us: They have the power of life and death. They will shape your kids' thinking and influence their future.

Make every one count.

INFLUENCING TIP #2:
Your words show your kids who you think they are, which shapes who they think they are. Use them wisely.

Consider:
Do you remember a time when someone's words powerfully impacted you, either positively or negatively? How powerful do you think your words are in the life of your kids? How can you use your words intentionally to influence how your kids think about themselves?

Chapter 13

Be a Fountain of Life

A proverb written almost three thousand years ago by King Solomon paints a powerful picture of the impact of words: "The mouth of the righteous is a fountain of life, but violence overwhelms the mouth of the wicked."[4] Let's put that verse into parent talk for a minute and it will read this way: The mouth of the righteous *parent* is a fountain of life *to his or her kids,* but violence overwhelms the mouth of the wicked *parent* (italics added).

Let the powerful message of this thought sink in for a minute. Picture a magical fountain of life, hidden deep in a remote jungle. Anyone who splashes around in it gets filled with a refreshing reservoir of new life. Injuries are healed and scars are washed away. Wrinkles are smoothed out and muscles rejuvenated. The wear and tear of hard years instantly erased. The clock is magically turned back.

The mouth of a parent—your mouth—can have the same effect on your kids. Your words can be a fountain of life to your children, rejuvenating them from the inside out. Giving them hope and vision they did not have the eyes to see. Helping them see past their limitations and failures. Your words can build your kids up, teach them, love them, encourage them, and guide them. Your words can leave your kids better off than before you spoke.

That's a fountain of life.

That's what God designed your mouth to be.

But what happens when a parent does not choose to use his or her words as a fountain of life? Damage and destruction follow. Careless and hurtful words echo in the deep recesses of a child's heart. Relational distance is created by his fear of being intimidated and put down. In the back of her mind is a nagging fear that her parent's low view of her might just be the truth.

Perhaps you know all too well what it is like to be on the receiving end of hurtful, negative words from a parent. You may have some of those words etched in a painful memory from your childhood that you'll never forget.

That is the last thing you want for your kids.

Consider this.

If there was a real fountain of life, would kids run away from it in fear? No, they'd run *toward* it with joy. They would play and splash around in it for hours. In fact, it would be hard to get them to leave and they would look forward to coming back.

When *your* words become a fountain of life, your kids will be refreshed and renewed by the life-giving and future-changing power of your words.

That's right. Your words.

Your kids will know they are loved and believed in. They will feel safe to make mistakes around you. They will be empowered by your belief and confidence in them. They will be more open to your guidance and direction because they will trust the source from which it comes. Your words will help your kids see themselves in relation to their Creator and learn to understand the dangers that lie outside of God's path. Your words will strengthen them when they face adversity and comfort them when they slip and fall. Your words will help your kids use their God-given imaginations to dream big, work hard, and be open to all God wants to do through them. As your kids get older, your words will help them begin to think through the difficult challenges and questions of life. Your life-giving words will echo in their memories for the rest of their lives.

How can your words become a fountain of life to your kids? They will when you

Encourage them.

Tell them what they are doing right (instead of just what they are doing wrong).

Point out their positive behaviors and characteristics.

Teach them how to solve problems and find solutions.

Remind them of God's love and faithfulness.

Correct them in a firm but gentle way.

Pray together often.

Frequently say that you love them and are proud of them.

Remember this: When your words become a fountain of life, your kids will run toward the source of those words.

They will run toward you.

INFLUENCING TIP #3:
Your words can be a fountain of life to your kids.

Consider:

Do you really think your words can be a fountain of life to your kids? If your words were honest, caring, thoughtful, uplifting, and encouraging, how would that draw your kids closer to you? How would that draw them closer to God?

Chapter 14

See More Than Meets the Eye

Alec is a four-year-old boy who was recently sent home for hitting and kicking the other kids at preschool. For the third time.

Cathleen is a six-year-old who can throw a fit with the best of them and does so on a regular basis. In fact, I remember helping her mom take Cathleen from my office to their car (she didn't want to leave, isn't that nice?) and watched her lying in the backseat of the car kicking at the car windows with all the might her little body could muster.

Ricky is a ten-year-old who takes great pleasure in intentionally annoying his sister. For instance, she doesn't like it when he whistles, so guess what his favorite new activity is?

And this is just my typical morning at work.

The parents of Alec, Cathleen, and Ricky have their work cut out for them. In this season of their family life, they have to deal with more disrespectful behavior and temper tantrums than the parents of less challenging kids usually do.

It is easy for them to fall into a common parenting trap, one that most of us slip into at some time or another, even if our kids are not as challenging as the three described above. The problem is that we are usually not aware we have fallen into the trap when we are actually tangled up by it.

What is this trap I am referring to?

Dirt-watching.

A story is told about author and positive thinking trainer extraordinaire Dale Carnegie, when he was once asked how he had managed to hire so many people who went on to become wildly financially successful. Carnegie answered with an illustration. He simply said that when you are mining for gold, you don't go into the mine looking for the dirt.

You go in looking for the gold.

As parents, we can learn a classic lesson from Dale Carnegie. We so easily get caught up in dirt-watching, because as we all know, there is plenty of dirt to watch. Getting up from the dinner table without being excused, arguing about turning off electronic games, sibling squabbles, getting mad about homework, refusing to go to bed—all of these behaviors can so easily consume our daily lives that we are simply on constant alert, just waiting for the next bit of dirt that we will have to deal with.

If we want to influence our kids, we need to see beyond the surface and remember that our kids are not little dirt clods at all. They are God's wonderful, handmade gold nuggets He has entrusted into our care. Our job is to help brush off the dirt on the outside and bring forth the wonderful gold nugget that lies just beneath the surface. Yes, some bits of dirt may take a little longer to remove and we may have to put some work into it. But we don't want to get so focused on the dirt that we forget to look for the gold.

I shared this idea of "looking for the gold" in a message I delivered one Sunday morning as a guest speaker at a church that was doing a parenting series. Both of our boys were there and for some reason this idea caught their attention. For the next several months they jokingly told each other to "be gold, not dirt," whenever one of them was close to getting in trouble. We all got a good laugh out of it, but they had clearly heard the message: Both of them always have the potential for "gold nugget" choices.

So how do you bring out the gold in your kids?

Watch for glimpses of gold nugget behaviors. Picture yourself in a poorly lit, dusty gold mine of yesteryear, chipping away at the dark, dirt walls with your pickax and constantly scanning for any signs of gold. Even a speck of gold immediately catches your attention. In the same way, keep your eyes peeled for glimpses of gold nugget behavior from your kids.

Listening when you ask them to do something (anything)
Playing nicely with a sibling
Working hard on homework
Taking turns
Getting ready for bed
Coming home on time
Saying "Thank you" for something

It is kind of like fishing in a pond that has been well stocked. You know the fish are in there somewhere. You just have to catch them. In the same way, you know that there is gold in "them thar hills." You just have to find it.

Dust off the gold with your attention. Nothing makes that gold shine like a little positive attention. When you see a glimpse of gold nugget behavior, immediately let your kids know that you saw it and appreciate it.

Repeat (and repeat and repeat). Any miner knows that where you find a bit of gold, a lot more is likely close by. Keep looking for gold nugget behaviors and dusting them off with your attention and appreciation. You will discover that you find a lot more gold when you look for it.

INFLUENCING TIP #4:

Your kids are God's gold nuggets.

The question is: Are you looking for the gold or the dirt?

Consider:

Do you find yourself slipping into the trap of focusing on the dirt instead of looking for the gold? How can you build the habit of looking for the gold in each of your kids?

Chapter 15

Find the Lesson

I remember one time when I was working on my computer on the main level of our home and our boys were playing a video game in the basement. All of a sudden, I heard the beginning of an angry commotion.

"Jake, stop it!"

"Luke, it's my turn!"

Something had gone awry in video game land.

I immediately got up and walked to the top of the basement stairs. I had no idea what exactly had happened; all I knew is that my boys were not handling things well. I called to them to stop the game and come to the bottom of the stairs where I could see them. They did and both of them were loudly talking over each other, trying to be first to tell me their side of the story.

Let's press the pause button right here.

As the dad, I had a couple of choices.

I could view this situation as an inconvenient intrusion and simply put an end to it. Or I could view this situation as a chance for the boys to learn a good lesson and use it.

Thankfully, on this occasion, I chose the second one.

So can you.

I'll have more to say about how to teach your kids the right lessons when we get to Tool #5, but for now I want to remind you that in any problem situation, there is always a lesson to teach. In this particular case, the lesson had to do with how to respectfully work out a problem regarding a video game. But learning that lesson starts with you.

If I had viewed this situation as simply an inconvenient problem to be stopped, I could have just told them that the video game was now over and they could each go to their rooms. Sound familiar? They would have learned that shouting loudly about video games was not a good idea, but that's where the learning would have stopped.

Instead, I looked at it as an opportunity to help my boys learn how to work through a problem they obviously needed some help handling.

That's okay, because that is exactly what I am there for.

So are you.

The point of this chapter is that in any problem situation you want to look for the lesson that you can help your kids learn. There is a lesson to be taught in virtually every situation:

Switching television channels while someone else is still watching a program

Refusing to share a toy (with the exception of special circumstances)

Purposely teasing or name-calling a sibling (or anyone for that matter)

Lying about homework

Cheating at a game

Expressing anger inappropriately

Now this is not to say that you stop every five minutes to give your kids a boring lecture about a lesson they need to learn. It just means that when correction is needed, you can use the language of "learning an important lesson" (about how to handle the situation the right way) to help them find a positive takeaway from the situation that will help them make a better choice in the future.

For example, in the scenario above, I had both boys stop talking for about twenty seconds and gave them time to think about what they wanted to say. Then I had them take turns telling me what happened, as long as they did it in a respectful way. We then switched gears into thinking together of a good idea for how to proceed from here. Both boys cooperated and the problem was solved fairly positively and quickly. We ended the conversation by highlighting two important lessons: There is always a way to communicate respectfully about a problem and, if we try, we can always find a good idea for how to handle a situation.

Would they have done any of that on their own?

I doubt it.

So when your kids lie about brushing their teeth, refuse to eat their vegetables, or quit a game because they are losing, ask yourself, "What lesson does my child need to learn from this situation?" The lesson may be:

To talk to Mom or Dad when they have a problem or are confused about something

To tell the truth when they have made a bad choice

They have to eat a few things that may not be their favorite
To say what they think or how they feel in a respectful way
They need to be flexible when things don't go their way (e.g.,
   Think: *I can handle it, it's no big deal*)

Your kids can learn each of these lessons. They need to learn each of these lessons. But they will only learn them if you turn problem situations into opportunities for positive lesson learning. Sometimes negative consequences will be involved, sometimes not. But either way, your kids will be glad they have a mom or dad who helped them find the lesson.

INFLUENCING TIP #5:
Your kids don't just have a negative
behavior to stop, they have an important lesson to learn.

Consider:
How does finding the lesson in any problem situation influence your kids? How will it help them learn to approach problems on their own?

TOOL #4
CONNECTING

Chapter 16

Use Your Touch

It was my junior year of high school and there I was, on the varsity football team. The only problem was that I had never played football before. Being from Canada, the only sport I was really familiar with was hockey, and my Southern California high school didn't have a hockey team.

Go figure.

A friend had talked me into joining the football team and there I was, decked out in full pads and a helmet. As a first-time player on the varsity team, the coaches put me at positions where I could do the least damage: a second string offensive guard and nose tackle. As I endured the grueling practices of double days in the summer and tried to work my way up to first string, I soon realized that I was probably destined to play second string for the entire year. Translation: Work hard in practices and probably never set foot in a real game.

The coaching staff consisted of a very thick and strong-looking head coach (I believe he had been a professional offensive lineman when he was younger) and a few assistant coaches, one of whom had an impressive arsenal of jokes, mostly rather off-color. While my illustrious football career spanned only one season, one moment stands out in my memory. It is a moment probably no other player noticed and not a soul on that team would recall except me.

But I remember it to this day.

We had just finished a practice in full pads and were walking through the regular locker room to the football locker room. You could hear the loud click-clack of dozens of cleats on the cement floor echoing through the locker room. As I walked with the team to the lockers, most of us too tired to talk much, I happened to walk past the head coach. Out of the blue, he slapped me a couple of times on the shoulder pads and declared, "Good job today, Cartmell!"

At that moment, perhaps for the first time, I felt like a football player. The coach had just slapped me on the shoulder pads!

Twice!

I was immediately aware of one thing. He didn't have to single me out. He didn't have to slap me on the pads. He chose to.

Touch is a powerful thing.

Whatever discouragement I had been feeling about a lack of playing time immediately took a backseat to the surge of hopefulness that rushed through me. *Maybe he thinks I'm improving. Maybe I actually did a good job in practice today. Maybe I can be a football player after all.*

That's a lot of mileage from a couple of slaps on the shoulder pads.

If a simple one-time slap on the pads from a coach was encouraging and connecting to this second-string high school football player, just imagine what kind of impact regular doses of warm touch from you will have on your kids. A hug, a kiss on the forehead, a pat on the back, a squeeze on the shoulder or knee, a high five—all these are powerful relationship builders. Why? Touching your kids communicates two powerful things:

I touched you intentionally. You don't get any credit for bumping into your kids or tripping over them on the way to the fridge. When you squeeze your kids on the shoulders, rub them on the back, or give them a high five, they know there was nothing accidental about it. You physically connected with them, and you did it on purpose. Intentionality builds close relationships.

I touched you because I love you. There is a hidden message inside each warm physical touch that comes from a parent: I love you. It is always there. It is never missed. Your kids instinctively know that you don't just go around touching and squeezing random people (or if you do, you'll likely receive a visit from a police officer before too long). You only touch those you are close to, or better yet, those you want to be close to. When you touch your kids, you are reminding them that you want to be close. This makes them feel loved and valued, which is exactly what they are.

I don't know where my head coach is today, but I do remember the encouraging impact he had on me that day on the way to the locker room. Your kids can have hundreds of such memories, each one making them feel noticed, appreciated, special, and loved.

And you don't even need cleats.

CONNECTING TIP #1:
Warm physical touch communicates to
your kids that you love them and want to be close to them.

Consider:

Do you think there is connecting power in physical touch? Does using physical touch to connect come naturally for you, or is this a habit you have to develop? How will regular, warm physical touch from you impact your family?

Chapter 17

Avoid the Time Trap

Sophia was a redheaded, eight-year-old girl who had a never-ending love for jumping on the trampoline and anything that was the color purple. The problem was that her dad, Jerry, didn't know this. In fact, Jerry didn't know a lot of things about Sophia.

Jerry loved his daughter, but had fallen into the trap of long hours at work, so he was exhausted by the time he arrived home. The result was that Jerry provided financially for his family but at the sacrifice of something even more valuable to him.

I have seen more than a few dads caught in this trap. The ironic thing is that they usually don't see it when it is happening. Like a lion slowly creeping up on its prey, the bottom-line demands of work stealthily demand more and more time and mental focus, depleting whatever mental energy might have been left for the family. It is a trap that, like the unwary antelope, we often don't see until it's too late.

Sophia sat on the comfortable blue couch in my office, looking at me with tears streaming down her face. "I never get to do anything with my dad anymore," she choked out. "We used to do stuff all the time when I was younger, but now he's always got to work."

Sophia and I talked about how much she enjoyed her times with her dad. Sophia recalled playing catch in the backyard and even going camping with Dad once. She lit up as she described Dad once helping her put together a new Lego set.

I asked Sophia if she had shared these feelings with her dad and she had not. I asked her if she wanted to and she did. So next session, we asked Jerry to join us and Sophia told her dad how she missed spending time together.

Jerry did not have an overly emotional reaction, but he did the one thing that counted: He listened. Then he acted. He told Sophia she was right; they had not been spending as much time together as they used to. Jerry acknowledged that he had gotten too busy with work and that he needed to change that.

Simple and straightforward.

I asked Sophia and Jerry to make a list of a few things they could start to do together, and it wasn't long before they had created a list with a variety of connecting activities, most small and a few big, that they could do together. The list included things as simple as talking at bedtime and playing a game of checkers after dinner, as well as a few more involved activities, such as another camping trip.

We kept expectations reasonable and goals practical. After all, Jerry still had a busy job and occasionally had to travel out of state for work. But the connection he had with his daughter Sophia had been reborn and both of them wanted to keep it that way.

If you want to revitalize your connection with your kids, or keep it strong and connected, you can. Here are a couple of things to keep in mind:

Quantity. There is no formula for how much quantity you need.

In fact, with the normal ebb and flow of life's demands, each week will probably be different from the week before. But a close relationship cannot be built or maintained without spending time together. You know this is true in your marriage and adult friendships, and it is true with your kids as well.

Quantity does not happen without intention, which is why it has relationship-connecting power. Time together might be as brief as a couple of minutes or as long as several hours. Perhaps you will check in with your kids after school, at meals, or at bedtime. Maybe you will spend some evening time playing games, reading, or praying together before bed. You may have a regular family time (which we will talk about later), or do fun activities together on the weekends. When your kids know you are making regular efforts to spend time with them, they will feel important to you and connected with you.

Quality. You can create countless ways to spend quality time with your kids. Talking in the car, playing a card game, shooting baskets, going to a concert, reading a book together, getting some ice cream, watching a television show, giving the dog a bath—any of these activities (and a thousand more) can be quality moments with your kids.

As we learned earlier, the one thing that turns time together into quality time together is when your kids know that you are more interested in them than in the activity. In other words, you *engage first* by asking questions about their life (e.g., school, activities, friends, sports, hobbies, recent situations, current challenges, things they are looking forward to).

You don't have to do this *every* time you do something with your kids; sometimes you will just be enjoying your activity together. But you want to do it many times. On top of this, you want to be connecting through use of body language, such as affirming touches on the arms and shoulders and lots of warm smiles. When you do this, any activity will become a powerful connecting activity.

Remember, Jesus didn't just do a little FaceTime or Skype with His disciples. He spent both quality and quantity time with them. When you engage first with your kids and do it on a regular basis, you also will have both quality and quantity.

And a connection is reborn.

Just ask Sophia.

CONNECTING TIP #2:
Close relationships need quality
interactions on a regular basis if you want them to stay close.

Consider:
In the midst of busy family life, how can you stay connected with your kids in terms of quality and quantity time?

Chapter 18

Get into Their World

It was a day I may never forget: The day I was introduced to the whimsical world of Mario Kart Double-Dash.

My boys, both college-aged mind you, were emotionally invested in a rousing game of Mario Kart Double-Dash. Luke was using a little mushroom-shaped character named Toadette as well as the Koopa Troopa (a turtle-type character), while Jake had elected to use Diddy-Kong (Donkey Kong's smaller monkey friend) and Bowser Jr., who I am told is the cute dragon child of Bowser.

Please don't ask me to explain any further; I don't think I can.

I sat beside our boys in our basement, watching them as they raced furiously around the entertainingly creative race courses, sped down treacherous shortcuts, and drove through translucent boxes that allowed them to pick up the devious devices and roadblocks they threw at each other. My older son, a senior in college, assured me that his roommate was virtually unbeatable at this game, a fact that his parents were no doubt very proud of.

If you are not familiar with this game, let me wager a guess that the target audience for this game is young boys somewhere between five and eight years old. As I sat there, trying to reassure myself that my boys' college education had not entirely gone to waste, the million-dollar question came from both of them at once: "Dad, do you want to play with us?"

My immediate thought was, *Ummm, no*. Now, I enjoy a good game of Madden as much as the next guy, but this game felt like a trip back to kindergarten. On top of that, I am basically terrible at racing games, so I know that I would provide absolutely no competition for my boys and would simply be fodder for the little booby traps they would be sending my way.

After a few seconds to reflect, my answer was yes.

I realized this was an invitation I could not pass up. Our older son, Jake, was graduating from college in a few days, moving twelve hours away to Pennsylvania to take a job as a worship pastor within a month, and getting married five months later. Our younger son, Luke, was wrapping up his associates degree at the local junior college and would transfer to Illinois State University next year.

I would be thrilled to play this game with them.

For as long as I can.

No matter what ages your kids are, you connect with them by getting into their world. If your child is into Legos, then so are you. If your kids are into playing house, then you are the butler, or the puppy, or whatever they want you to be. A father and young son in our neighborhood can often be seen playing hockey in their driveway. They set up a net and the son practices his shots while Dad feeds him the pucks along with plenty of encouragement. I don't know what that dad thinks about hockey, but I do know that he is getting into his son's world.

Your goal is not to take over or micromanage your child's activities, but simply to learn enough about them to enjoy them with your child, help your child as needed, and provide love and encouragement. I talked with a father one day and asked him what he and his son enjoyed doing together. He matter-of-factly said that they didn't do much together because his son was into computers and he was not. I remember thinking sadly that this father had entirely missed the point. One of these days, his chance to connect with his son will be gone and he will wish he had the chance to turn back the clock and learn about computers along with him.

What are your kids into today? What important events are happening in their world? Is it playing with dolls or stuffed animals? The release of a new video game? Is it the speech/debate club at school? Is your child into gymnastics or dance? Does your child love art or music? How about reading? Does your child have a big project on the Amazon jungle she needs help researching? I met a boy yesterday who told me that he loves building things. I immediately wondered if his mom or dad builds things with him.

When you get into your child's world, you are showing them that what is important to them is important to you. No matter how little or big, how in or out of your range, your child's world is important to you because she or he is important to you.

Every child wants to be connected with their parents.

This means that your kids want to be connected with you.

If you want to be close with your kids, then get into their world and let the connecting begin.

CONNECTING TIP #3:
When you get into your child's world,
they know you are doing it because you love them.

Consider:

What is one way you can get into the world of each of your kids?

Chapter 19

Learn Together

When Luke was in middle school, he was into basketball. So he and I shot baskets and played HORSE and one-on-one countless times at the nearby elementary school basketball court. To do this with at least a minimal level of competence, I had to pay attention to the instruction from his practices and apply it to myself, so I knew the right form for free throws, jump shots, and so on.

In other words, I had to take a refresher course in basketball.

Jake, on the other hand, got into karate, so he, Luke, and I signed up (Lora also, until her knees couldn't take it anymore) for parent/child karate classes. Karate was a blast and we all enjoyed learning, practicing kata and kumite (sparring) in our basement, and competing in tournaments (the boys took great joy in reminding me that I was in the senior division).

In other words, I had to learn some karate.

Looking back, some of our best experiences and memories came from times when we didn't just do things together, we learned things together. Learning together is different from simply doing an activity together. For example, playing a game of Monopoly together is fun, but you generally know what the game is like and that it is going to end with someone winning and everyone else trying not to lose their shirt in bankruptcy.

On the other hand, when you are learning together, it is kind of like going on a camping trip for the first time. You kind of know what to expect (tent, lots of trees, hopefully no bears), but everything has a fresh sense of adventure, excitement, and newness. You don't know exactly what you are going to find on the trail because you have never been on this trail before. Better yet, you are sharing this new experience together, making wonderful memories you will always share.

What is something that you can learn about with your kids? The answer will depend on the ages of your kids as well as their interests. Here are some ideas:

Learn how to play a certain game (darts, chess, badminton)
Learn about a country
Learn about their favorite animal
Learn about magic tricks
Learn about a topic of interest or a certain historical event or
    period together and create a presentation for your family
Learn how to play a sport that you both enjoy
Learn how to make/build/sew something
Learn how something works (clock, computer)
Learn how to cook a meal or bake a treat

Learning together involves reading, getting information from the library or online, trying things, making mistakes, learning from those mistakes, and trying again. Your kids get to see you mess up and they will observe and learn from how you respond to your mistakes.

As our boys entered their teen years, we began to discuss more adult-level questions about the Christian faith and we decided to learn together about issues such as the historical reliability of the Bible, the problem of pain and suffering, evolution and intelligent design, alternative religions and worldviews, and so on. We have read books, listened to radio/TV programs, and watched YouTube videos together as we have explored these issues that are so central to a credible and intellectually defendable faith.

Not only have we grown in our knowledge of these topics, we have also grown in our relationship with one another.

Learning together tends to do that.

I encourage you to talk with your kids today and find something you can learn about together. It will be an adventure you will treasure for the rest of your life.

And so will your kids.

CONNECTING TIP #4:
Learning together creates shared experiences
and memories in a way that you and your kids
will treasure for a lifetime.

Consider:

What is one thing you have learned about along with your kids? What did it do for your relationship? What is another idea for something you can learn about together?

Chapter 20

Have a Regular Family Time

One Saturday evening, our family was sitting together in our living room. I had taken a sheet of notebook paper, turned it long ways, and drawn a rough sketch of a thermometer, with the number 10 on the top, 5 in the middle, and 1 on the bottom. For our discussion, this illustration was going to be our "Respect Thermometer."

Every family could use a Respect Thermometer now and then.

I showed Lora and the boys my masterpiece and asked, "How are we doing at treating one another respectfully in our family?"

Each of us took a turn at giving our family a rating and explaining why we chose that number. Then we talked about some of the ways we all treated each other respectfully and ways we all could improve. We talked about how God wanted us to show proper respect to each other[1] and look out for others' interests, not just our own.[2] We closed our discussion with a time of prayer (each person praying for the person on their left) and then watched a fun movie together.

Of all the parenting decisions Lora and I have made in our life, the decision to have a regular family time is easily the smartest one.

Hands down.

An effective family time has two components: a fun activity and meaningful discussion. The order does not matter. A fun activity is simply something you all enjoy doing together. Besides watching a movie, we have played a board or card game, decorated cookies, gone to the park, camped in the backyard, played miniature golf, got some ice cream, visited the zoo, and so on. The important thing is that you are spending time together, enjoying each other's company, building your relationships, and creating lasting memories.

As much fun as this was, my favorite part of the family time was always the second component: meaningful discussion. During this part of your family time, you take ten to twenty minutes and talk about something important. You have many different choices. Some of our discussions have included:

Reading through age-appropriate devotional books

Talking about recent family happenings (e.g., starting a new school year)

Discussing the highs and lows of the week for each of us

Talking about our current friends and how we can influence and pray for them

Working through a family issue/problem together such as sharing toys

Thinking together about the importance of keeping a healthy balance with electronic activities (television, video games, etc.)

Teaching/practicing a family skill (how to solve a problem, how to talk to each other)[3]

Taking inventory on how we are doing as a family
Making our list of family dos and don'ts (and writing it down)
Deciding what kind of family we want to be

Our family times would then end with a time of prayer. Sometimes one of us would say a closing prayer, but more often, we all would pray. Frequently, we would go around in a circle, praying for the person on our right or left.

Do you see why I love family times? These discussions have been some of the best we have ever had. They bonded us close together, created a warm relational atmosphere, and helped us work through problems and family issues from a biblical perspective in a way that made big problems smaller and gave us a framework for handling day to day issues in a respectful way.

For instance, I can remember listening to my young boys tell me about their current list of friends and thinking together about how they can be a positive and godly influence in their lives. I remember our going around in a circle and saying things we appreciate about the person on our left or right (and actually being able to come up with some). I remember talking about how God made each of us special and different and thinking about the unique gifts and talents that He has given each of us and how we can encourage each other in these areas.

Just recalling these discussions brings tears to my eyes even now.

Every one of these discussions can happen in your family as well.

Here's the zinger: I am absolutely convinced that these powerful and bonding family time discussions would not have happened if we had not developed the habit of a regular family time. One or two of them could have possibly spontaneously occurred, I suppose. But not all of them. The busy hustle and bustle of everyday life impedes meaningful, reflective discussions. It is only when you cultivate the regular habit of stopping and reflecting together on the things that are important that you get this kind of interaction on a regular basis.

Do you want a transformed family?

Then give your kids the gift of a regular family time.

CONNECTING TIP #5:
A regular family time is one of the most powerful
tools you can use to build a close and connected family.

Consider:

What impact can a regular family time have on your family? What are three topics that would make for good family time discussions? What are some activities you can do during these times?

TOOL #5
TEACHING

Chapter 21

Emphasize Respect

I was recently talking with eleven-year-old Greg. It turned out that he was developing a habit of arguing with and talking back to his parents. I had the sense that Greg knew this was wrong, so I asked him a simple question.

"Greg, when is it important to be respectful?"

He hit it on the nose. "All the time."

Greg instinctively knew the truth of Jesus' command for us to "do to others as you would have them do to you."[1] At that point, I shared with Greg something that I have come to call the Family Respect Rule.[2] It goes like this:

**Everyone in our family should treat
everyone else in our family respectfully.
All the time.**

"Well, what do you think?" I asked Greg. "Do you like it?"

"Yep," came his reply, similar to every other child or teenager I have shared the Family Respect Rule with.

The Family Respect Rule is made up of three main points that will transform your kids and family, so I don't want you to miss them. Let me share them in question form.

QUESTION #1: *Who does the Family Respect Rule apply to?* **Answer:** Everyone. As a parent, you know that "everyone" includes your kids but it begins with you. There should not be any other person in your family who works harder to keep the Family Respect Rule than you.

Nobody.

QUESTION #2: *When does the Family Respect Rule apply?* **Answer:** All the time. Here's an interesting thing: All the time really means all the time. This is saying that there is never a time when it is okay to hurt someone in your family with your words or actions. It is not okay with me if one of my sons does it; it is not okay with me if I do it. When you are happy, when you are sad, when you are joking, when you are mad, in the morning, in the evening, when you are tired from work, when there are chores to do, when you win, when you lose . . . get the idea? Now, I must point out that no one will keep the Family Respect Rule perfectly; we all will blow it from time to time. But "all the time" is the bar you reach for.

QUESTION #3: *What is the basis for the Family Respect Rule?* **Answer:** And here's the part I love the most. Everyone in your family was made by who? God. Everyone in your family is of great value to who? To God and, of course, to you. So what do you do with things that are of great value to you? Do you kick them around or toss them into the dirt? Of course not. You handle them gently, take care of them, and keep them in a safe place. Everyone in your family is valuable and precious and we want to protect them and nurture them, not damage them. In other words, you treat them with a great deal of . . . (here it comes) . . . respect.

There are other obvious reasons to follow the Family Respect Rule as well:

You want to build a close relationship with your kids.
You want to be a parent your kids will talk to and listen to.
You want your kids to be open to your guidance.
You want your kids to learn to be respectful from your example.

None of these things happen without a respectful and loving style from Mom and Dad. They just don't.

Eleven-year-old Greg knew this.

So do your kids.

So do you.

How do you teach the Family Respect Rule to your kids?

Read and discuss the Family Respect Rule together. Using the three points explained above, explain to your kids who it applies to, when it applies, and why.

Identify ways you can treat each other respectfully. Make a list of respectful behaviors you can all do. Talking calmly, no shouting, listening to parents, playing together in a friendly way, and so on. Put the list somewhere where everyone can see it.

Follow the Family Respect Rule yourself. Show your kids that you really mean what you say. Let them see you follow the Family Respect Rule better than they do.

Enforce and check in. Make sure your kids clearly experience that when they handle a situation respectfully, they will be in good shape. It is when they choose to be disrespectful that negative consequences will quickly arrive at their doorstep. Also, make it a point (in your family times) to check in and get everyone's opinion as to how your family is doing at following the Family Respect Rule and where things can be improved.

You may even find yourself making a Respect Thermometer for a family time as previously described. If you do, know that your family is on the road toward becoming a more respectful family. It may take some work and time, but you can get there if you stick with it. And the best thing of all is that you are leading the way.

TEACHING TIP #1:
**When you follow the Family Respect Rule
and teach it to your kids, your family will never be the same.**

Consider:

How do you think your kids will respond to the Family Respect Rule? If you introduce it, talk about it together, model it, enforce it, and revisit it in your family times, how will it impact your family?

Chapter 22

Practice Positive Behavior

Kayla is a twelve-year-old girl who constantly forgets to put her backpack in the right place when she comes home from school. Despite her mother's constant requests that she put her backpack elsewhere, Kayla just drops it in the middle of the floor. Mysterious.

Tyler is a nine-year-old boy who frequently whines and complains when it is time to brush his teeth. Sometimes he will even stand in the bathroom, run the water, and pretend that he has brushed his teeth. A simple breath test usually reveals the truth.

Any of this ever happened with your kids?

A little yelling about it has probably not done the trick.

A little practice will.

Here's the idea. Kids learn things all the time. They learn how to read, how to play an instrument, or how to play soccer, for instance. Kids *don't* learn how to play soccer by having the coach sit down on the grass and explain the mechanics of kicking and passing a soccer ball while they blankly stare at the sky. They *do* learn through a combination of instruction and practice. We see this every day. The soccer coach will explain how to pass the ball and then he will follow that up with a chance for the kids to practice. It is when they *practice* that the new skill begins to take root.

As parents, we are pretty familiar with the instruction part, but that is usually where we stop. We typically don't take the next step and *practice* the positive behavior we want our kids to learn.

So here's how you do it:

Develop a simple plan. Pick a problem situation, like either of the two above, and figure out what you want your kids to say and do in that situation. Keep it simple and put the steps in logical order. For example, with Kayla, we came up with this simple plan:

1. Walk in the door.
2. Put her backpack on the chair Mom had chosen.

That's it. But that is exactly what her mom wanted her to do.

Here's the plan we came up with for Tyler when he was asked to brush his teeth:

1. Tyler is reminded it's time to brush his teeth; he says, "Okay," and immediately goes into the bathroom.
2. He puts toothpaste on his brush and sets a timer for sixty seconds.
3. He brushes until the timer dings.

Get the idea? Simple plans for what to say and do in a situation.

Practice the plan together. Here's the step you probably have not done before. Just like a soccer coach, you are going to practice this new plan with your kids. Not in a real situation, but in a pretend situation. After all, that's what practice is. A scrimmage is not a real game, it is a practice, where kids have a chance to build their skills before the real game.

Here's how we did it with Kayla. We told her that continuing to put her backpack in the middle of the entryway (where Mom had asked her not to put it) was not only disrespectful to Mom but inconsiderate toward others who now had to move her backpack or step around it. This behavior would certainly result in significant privilege loss, which would be very sad for Kayla. However, to help her avoid these negative consequences, Mom was willing to help her learn to put her backpack in the right place with no negative consequences at all.

That's quite a deal.

So one Saturday morning, Mom went over the plan with Kayla. Then she had her fill up her backpack with schoolbooks, go outside, and then walk in, say hi, and place her backpack on the right chair. Kayla did it like a pro and Mom gave her a little hug. Then she did it again. And again. And again. Ten times in a row.

Practice was over. Until tomorrow, when they went through it again, this time about seven more times. And the next day, six more times.

Kayla had now practiced her new plan close to twenty-five times. I think she was getting the idea. Mom now told her that if she put her backpack away properly when she came home from school, she wouldn't need to practice anymore. But if she "forgot," then they could do another five to ten repetitions to help her remember.

Backpack problem solved.

No shouting, no screaming. Just a little practice. If Kayla had refused to practice, Mom would have told her that a certain privilege (parent's choice) would be discontinued until she agreed.

This approach fits best for daily household routines, such as bedtime or morning routines, putting toys away, placing dirty clothes in the hamper, etc. All you need to do is come up with a simple plan for what you want your kids to say and do, go over it clearly, and practice it together. Problem solved and often no negative consequences required.

Just a little practice.

TEACHING TIP #2:
Practicing positive behavior together
helps your kids develop good habits to replace the bad ones.

Consider:

What is a simple positive behavior that your child needs to improve at? How would you break it down into simple steps? What effect do you think practicing it will have?

Chapter 23

Teach Flexible Thinking

Jennifer sat across from me in my office, looking somewhat deflated, telling me about her fourteen-year-old daughter, Chloe. She started by telling me that Chloe was a wonderful girl who could be caring, funny, and delightful to be around.

"*So far, so good*," I thought.

"The problem is when she doesn't get her way," Jennifer continued. "Chloe will be rude, talk back, and get really mad. She basically throws a big fit, kind of like a five-year-old. I am starting to see the same thing when she is playing with her sister and with her friends. She only wants to do things her way."

"Kind of bossy?" I asked.

"Yes, exactly," Jennifer replied. "She comes off as bossy and controlling. She has a hard time accepting someone else's ideas for how to do things."

I met Chloe a week later and she was exactly as Jennifer had described: friendly, pleasant, and easy to talk with. In my office that is. As we talked, Chloe admitted that she often became angry over small things, which got her in a lot of trouble at home. She even showed some awareness that this bad habit was starting to affect her friendships.

Chloe needed to learn how to be more flexible.

Maybe your kids do too.

Flexible thinking is an important life skill. The way your kids think influences how they feel and act in any situation. You may recall that the apostle Paul tells us to be made "new in the attitude of your minds."[3] Thinking in a biblically accurate way helps us to make wise and godly decisions in all areas of our lives and treat others the way we would like to be treated. When a situation doesn't go the way your kids are hoping for (they have to stop playing a video game, it is time to do homework or chores), it is easy for their minds to become overrun by *mad* thoughts (e.g., "That's not fair!" "I never get to do it!" "It will take forever!"). When your child's mad thoughts prevail, anger boils over, and disrespectful words and actions are usually not far behind. The end result: She handles the situation poorly and gets in big trouble. When the mad thoughts win, your child loses.

Instead, flexible thoughts (e.g., "It's no big deal," "It will really help Mom if I put these dishes away," "Things don't always have to be just the way I want") will help your kids put a situation into an accurate perspective and respond much more respectfully in everyday situations. Here is how you get the process started:[4]

Teach your kids the Top Five list. Tell your kids that when things don't go their way, they can think in either a mad way or a flexible way. Mad thoughts will lead to anger and make it easier to make a disrespectful or unfriendly choice. Flexible thoughts will help them stay calm and find it easier to make a respectful or friendly choice. You are going to give them a "starter pack" of flexible thoughts. Here is the Top Five list I have taught to hundreds of kids:

I should just do it.

It's no big deal.

It won't take that long.

The sooner I start, the sooner I'm done.

That's okay, I can do it later.

Review this list with your kids until they have the flexible thoughts memorized. It is always a nice touch if you memorize them too.

Do scenario practice. Once the Top Five list has been learned, help your child build her flexible skills by applying flexible thoughts to practice scenarios like this:

Parent: "Let's pretend that Mom asks you to hang up your clean clothes. Which flexible thought will help you make a good choice?" (What should you think, or say to yourself?)

Chloe: "I should just do it."

Parent: "Great. Let's try another one. Let's pretend that you are playing a video game and it is time to stop. What flexible thought will help you make a good choice?" (What should you think, or say to yourself?)

Chloe: "It's no big deal or That's okay, I can play it later."

Parent: "Nice job. Can you make up one of your own?"

Chloe: "Ummm, It's just a game and I guess it's not going anywhere."

You can practice home, school, and peer scenarios.[5] When you regularly practice flexible thinking with your kids, the Top Five list will gradually work its way into their thought patterns and have a remarkable effect on how they handle situations that don't go their way. It may take a bit of time, and negative consequences will still be needed in certain situations, of course. But every time something doesn't go their way, there is a flexible thought that will help your kids make a good choice.

You are helping them learn to find it.

TEACHING TIP #3:
Flexible thinking will help your kids treat
others the way they would like to be treated in any situation.

Consider:
How flexible are your kids? What impact will it have if you memorize and practice the Top Five list with your kids?

Chapter 24

Find the Solution

I locked my office door and told ten-year-old Peter to stand outside the door and try to get in. He just stood there, a tad confused. I suggested that he bang on the door or kick it a few times. He did, rather hesitantly. It didn't open. After letting him stand there a little longer, I tossed him my bulky set of keys and told him that the key to open the door was on the key ring.

It was up to him to find the right one.

He randomly picked one and tried to turn it. It didn't work; it was too small. This time, he more carefully sized them up and chose one that looked like it would be the right size. No luck. Was I tricking him?

"It's on there," I reassured him.

He kept trying until he found the one that opened the door.

With a little effort and encouragement, Peter had solved the problem.

Peter opened the door and sat down, and we talked about what had just taken place. He had been faced with a problem: a locked office door. He could have shouted at the door or banged on it, but that would not have opened it. Even when he had the keys, the first key he tried didn't work. Neither did the second one. He could have gone back to banging on the door, but that wouldn't have helped. It was only when he persisted in trying to find a good solution that he found the key that opened the door.

Your kids are faced with problems on a daily basis.

A sibling changing the TV channel while the other is watching a
    program
Striking out in a baseball game
Trying to master a difficult gymnastics move
Solving a difficult math problem
Wanting a new video game that parents say is either too expensive
    or age-inappropriate

Life leaves us with no shortage of problems. The question is whether your kids will choose from the good idea basket or the bad idea basket. Proverbs tells us, "The wisdom of the prudent is to give thought to their ways, but the folly of fools is deception."[6] We want our kids to learn to give thought to their ways when faced with situational problems that arise as well as big life issues.

You can help your kids learn to do just that. Here's how:

Teach them problem-solving steps. The acronym STEPS can be used to remember these five steps:

Stop (stop what you are saying and doing until you know it will be
    helpful. Taking a deep breath is a great way to stop
    and it paves the way for moving onto the next step).

Think of possible solutions (list as many as you can—good
   or bad).

Evaluate the solutions (decide if you think they will be helpful or
   not).

Pick a solution (choose one or more to try).

See if it worked (after you have used your solution, determine if
   it was helpful or not. If it was, remember it for next time. If it
   was not, try a different solution).

Practice the STEPS on sample problems. Make up a few easy
problems and practice going through the steps with your kids. Sample
problems might include a child misplacing a baseball glove, getting
stuck on a homework problem, or two siblings wanting to watch different television shows at the same time. Walk your kids through the steps
in order, taking time to hear all their ideas and helping them figure out
which ones would work the best.

Look for opportunities to use the STEPS in real life. You won't
have to wait long for this one. When a real problem pops up, your
kids will now be better prepared to look for good ideas, but will still
need your help. The moment you see them respond with a bad idea
(e.g., yelling, arguing, quitting), get in there and help them use their
STEPS. They will be tempted to focus on what someone else did or why
something is so unfair, but help them slow the situation down and talk
through the STEPS calmly and thoughtfully.

"What is the problem?"

"What is a good way to stop so that you can think?"

"What are some ideas for what you can do? What are some good
   ideas? What are some bad ideas?"

"What would happen if you [name an idea]? Do you think this is a
good idea or a bad idea?"

"Which idea (or combination) do you think will work the best?"

"Let's try it and see how it works."

Problem-solving skills will take time and practice for your kids to
master. On occasion, your kids may be too flustered to use their STEPS.
That's okay; do your best to help them make a good choice on the spot
and go over the situation with them later, when they have calmed
down. Either way, the process of learning to stop and give thought to
their ways is a skill that will benefit your kids both now and throughout
their adult life.

As Peter learned, it is much better than kicking a locked door.

TEACHING TIP #4:
Every problem has one or more
good solutions. Your kids can learn to find them.

Consider:
*How will using the problem-solving STEPS help your kids learn to
handle life's challenges in a way that obeys Jesus' command for us to
treat others as we would like to be treated?*

Chapter 25

Solve Problems on the Spot

I t was a sunny Saturday afternoon as Wendy took her seven-year-old son, Mark, to the toy store to get a birthday gift for his older brother, who was turning nine the following week. Mark was excited as he looked at the never-ending assortment of games, action figures, and building sets.

Then it happened.

Mark's eyes fell on a muscular Batman action figure. In all his years, he had never seen its equal. Criminals would surely have no choice but to flee from this intimidating crime-fighting specimen. He had to have it.

"Mom, can I get it, pleeeeeeease?" he asked.

"Sorry, honey," came the reply, "we are only getting a toy for Billy today. You have lots of action figures at home."

The groundswell of disappointment that came over Mark was something that only a superhero-loving kid could understand. He fell to the floor in utter anguish, not caring who might notice, devastated that a mere mortal power (i.e., his mother) would dare stand between him and his newfound comrade in crime prevention.

In other words, he threw a tantrum.

When a tantrum really gets rolling, it is hard for a child to think rationally. I'm guessing you have run into this before. You can suggest a flexible thought in your nicest voice, but he may not take the bait. The chance of calmly walking your child through the problem-solving steps when he is in tantrum mode is also not a bet they would take in Vegas. When you are in a difficult situation like this, try to avoid the trap of worrying about what the other parents around you may be thinking. Instead, focus on one thing: Doing your job as best as you can. What is your job in that moment? Trying to help your child calm down and find a good solution.

Luckily, you have a secret weapon that will help you do just that. I call it problem solving on-the-go. It can be very effective in helping a child who is headed for a tantrum to quickly switch course. There are two simple steps and they must be done in order:

Make an empathic comment. When kids are getting angry about having to do homework or having to stop a fun activity, they expect you to quickly repeat your request, in an even firmer tone. In fact, this is what you would usually do. However, if you sense that your child's clear thinking is becoming overwhelmed by a flood of angry emotions, then it is time to throw them a helpful curveball.

You are simply going to make an empathic comment. "What is an empathic comment?" you might ask. It is a comment that calmly describes how your child is feeling at that moment, so they know that you really understand where they are coming from. The trick is that you are not *telling* them to do anything, so they have nothing to argue about. It might sound like this:

"Mark, it looks like you really like that Batman toy. I know it is really disappointing to not be able to get something that seems so cool."

"Paige, it sounds like you really don't want to do your homework right now. I sure understand. When I was in school, there were a lot of times I didn't feel like doing my homework either."

When you make an empathic comment that accurately captures your child's feelings at that moment, all they can say is, "Yeah, that's right." Good. Now they know that you understand how they feel, and their defenses have lowered a bit. You are ready for the next step.

Engage them in mutual problem solving. Again, you are not giving any commands, so there is nothing for your child to argue with. Simply try to engage them in problem solving by asking, "Well, what do *you* think would be a good idea?" You can phrase it any way you like, but you are asking your kids for *their* opinion, for *their* ideas.

For example, after making her empathic comment, Wendy might calmly and softly ask, "Pal, what do you think we should do?"

"I want that Batman!" Mark might stubbornly reply.

"Well, we are here to get a toy for Billy today, remember?" Wendy could say.

"But I want Batman." Mark holds his ground.

"That Batman is pretty cool. Can I see it?" Wendy admires the toy, giving Mark a little more time to settle down. "Well, this is a very nice Batman. It looks like he could get a lot of bad guys. Let's think about our choices." She pauses, intentionally slowing the conversation. "Our job today is to find a toy for Billy. If you throw a fit about the Batman toy, do you think we will probably get it?"

"No," Mark admits.

"That's right. But if we get Billy's toy today and if you stay calm, do you think there is any way that we could maybe get this Batman some other time?" Wendy asked.

"Maybe tomorrow?" Mark asked.

"Well, maybe. We'll have to talk about it. But right now you have to decide if you want to throw a tantrum or stay calm. It's up to you."

Notice that Wendy gave no commands during that discussion. She simply made an empathic response and then helped Mark move into problem-solving mode. Of course, sometimes, despite your best efforts, your child will just throw a tantrum and you have to load him into the car and go home. But more times than not, problem solving on-the-go will redirect the conversation in a productive direction.

A problem solved is a tantrum avoided. That's a good day, even for a superhero.

TEACHING TIP #5:
An empathic response can open the door to
mutual problem solving and turn a situation around.

Consider:
Can you think of a situation where problem solving on-the-go would have been helpful? What difference does an empathic response make?

TOOL #6
ENCOURAGING

Chapter 26

Point Out Positive Behaviors

There is one parenting idea I have included in every one of my books. Why? Running out of material? Nope. Cutting corners? Nope. Lazy? Hmmm, you'd have to ask my wife about that.

My answer is that this idea is simply that important.

So here it is.

Again.

Andrew was a ten-year-old boy who was brought to me because of his tendency to argue, complain, and refuse to do what his parents asked. He had been doing this for about . . . ten years (rim shot, please). After meeting with Andrew's parents once, then Andrew a few times, I got together with his parents again and taught them how to effectively point out positive behaviors. Within three weeks, Andrew's behavior had shown about a 70 percent improvement.

Stop and think about that for a moment.

Are you salivating yet? (Psychology humor!)

Truth in advertising—not all kids improve as quickly as Andrew. Some improve even faster. And a few slower. But I can't think of one who hasn't improved as the result of Mom and Dad learning to effectively point out positive behavior.

The truth is that most of you reading this book are *not* pointing out your kids' positive behavior as effectively as you can. Strange as it may seem, this is actually good news. Why? Just think about what will happen when you *are* pointing out your kids' positive behavior as effectively as you can. You have something to look forward to.

Proverbs 16:24 tells us, "Gracious words are a honeycomb, sweet to the soul and healing to the bones." You are about to discover that gracious, pleasant words have a pretty good effect on positive behavior as well. We are going to take the idea we discussed of looking for the gold and put it on steroids. To do this you must think of yourself not only as a parent but as a trainer. You are helping your kids develop good habits and leave the bad habits behind. That is training. And a good trainer knows how to point out positive behavior. Here's how you do it:

Pick a positive behavior. You may choose whatever positive behavior you like, but make it clear and easily observable. For instance, you may choose doing what you ask the first time, being flexible when a situation doesn't go their way, playing cooperatively with a sibling, following the morning/bedtime routine, and so on.

Watch very carefully for that behavior to happen. Sounds obvious, but it is easy to mess up this step. If we were to record you (and your kids) on a random day, we would probably find that you are pointing out only a very *small* percentage of your kids' positive behavior.

No way, you say. Yes way.

One of the keys to effectively increasing a positive behavior is to respond to a high percentage of the positive behavior you are trying to increase. This means you have to be *on the lookout* for that behavior. You have to watch for it like a hawk. Keep in mind that the behavior doesn't have to be demonstrated perfectly at the start. For example, if your kids can't play together for ten minutes without fighting, then watch for them to play for five minutes without bickering. If your child goes to start her homework when you asked but shows a little bit of a grumpy attitude, remember that she has still chosen to do what you asked, just not perfectly. Find some level of positive behavior to point out. You can always "raise the bar" later.

Immediately follow the positive behavior by positively describing it and, when possible, add physical touch. A positive description simply means that you are going to tell your kids exactly what they said or did that you liked so much and you are going to do it in a very encouraging way. Add plenty of detail. For example, let's say you ask Justin to turn off the TV and get ready for bed and he did it.

Pretty Good—Parent: "Good job, Justin."

Incredibly Effective—Parent: "Hey, pal, I just asked you to turn off the TV and get ready for bed and you said, 'Okay, Dad,' and hopped up to do it right away. Justin, that was great listening the first time. I really appreciate that, buddy. Awesome job!" (add a high five).

Always try to add a little bit of warm physical touch, like a squeeze on the shoulder or knee, a high five, or something similar. As we have previously discussed, warm physical touch is a powerful reward and relationship builder, and this is the perfect time to use it.

I cannot tell you how many children and teens I have seen whose behavior has been positively changed when parents learn how to effectively point out positive behavior. Research has demonstrated this to be one of the most effective things a parent can do to turn negative behavior around.

As the proverb points out, pleasant words are powerful and you have a never-ending supply.

ENCOURAGING TIP #1:
Consistently pointing out positive
behavior is a powerful way to transform your child's habits.

Consider:

How would you rate yourself on a 1–10 scale (10 best) at regularly pointing out your kids' positive behaviors? How can you remind yourself to do it more consistently? What difference do you think it will make?

Chapter 27

Point Out
Positive Traits

I f you liked the last chapter, you might like this one even better.

Why? Because everyone likes to be encouraged. Everyone needs to be encouraged. This includes your kids. The writer of Hebrews tells us: "Encourage one another daily, as long as it is called 'Today,' so that none of you may be hardened by sin's deceitfulness."[1]

As we pointed out before, your kids need your daily encouragement to remember who they are and who they can become. They are God's handiwork[2] and we don't want them to forget it. They are imperfect, they make mistakes, and they make sinful choices, as do all of us. But no matter how challenging their behavior may be, God has a wonderful purpose and intention for their lives; He wants to do great things of eternal value through them. He wants them to develop traits that reflect His character, such as love, joy, peace, patience, kindness, goodness, faithfulness, gentleness, and self-control.[3]

Your daily encouragement can help that happen.

One day, I asked our younger son, Luke, to bring down his laundry basket so we could get some clothes washed. He went upstairs and pretty soon came down with his basket, filled and overflowing with dirty clothes. My options:

(1) Say nothing.
(2) Say "Thanks."
(3) Point out the positive behavior: "Luke, thanks for bringing your laundry down so quickly. I appreciate it."
(4) Point out the positive behavior and the positive underlying trait: "Luke, thanks for bringing your laundry down. That was really *helpful*."

While (2) above is good and (3) is great, (4) is even better. If you think about it, every positive behavior displays an underlying characteristic or trait, even if it is in the embryonic stage. For example, if Emma spends thirty minutes working on her homework, what trait would you say that positive behavior displays?

Possible answers: hardworking, diligent, perseverance, flexibility, self-control.

Not bad for a half-hour of homework.

When you point out Emma's positive behavior, you can also verbalize the positive trait that lies *underneath* that behavior. You don't have to use fancy words like perseverance; in fact, I always like to say things in the simplest possible way. For Emma, it might sound like this:

Parent: "Emma, I noticed that you've been working really hard on your homework for a long time today (as you squeeze her on the shoulder). I know homework is not always the most fun thing, so nice job sticking with something important, even if it's not always that fun to do."

Emma: "Thanks!"

Do you see what just happened? Emma now knows three things:

You noticed her positive behavior.

You took the time to point it out.

You think she is the kind of girl who sticks with important things, even when they are not that fun.

Perhaps Emma had not really thought of herself that way before.

She does now.

We've talked about how powerful your words are to your kids. Your words show your kids who you think they are, which shapes who they think they are and who they think they can become. Repeated thousands of times, your words can literally change the trajectory of your kids' lives.

That's what happens when you point out your kids' positive traits.

What kind of positive traits might you be looking for? Here's a list to start with:

Honest	Funny	Loyal
Hardworking	Smart	Generous
Caring	Joyful	Polite
Respectful	Thoughtful	Considerate
Friendly	Diligent	Encouraging
Supportive	Organized	Flexible
Compassionate	Outgoing	Warm
Helpful	Focused	Forgiving
God-honoring	Fun	Creative

Find a few traits in the above list that you see growing in your kids. Then watch for them and point them out as often as possible. Your daily encouragement will shape how your kids think about themselves and help them recognize that they are becoming the young men and women God has designed them to be.

ENCOURAGING TIP #2:
When you point out your kids' positive traits each day, you help them see the person God is helping them become.

Consider:
When you take it one step further and point out your kids' positive character traits, how will these affirming words shape them, both now and in the future?

Chapter 28

Water the *Whole* Lawn Regularly

Walking out to my car one warm summer morning as I was preparing to head off to work, I noticed my next door neighbor carefully positioning her sprinkler in the middle of her lawn.

It seems rather early to be watering the grass, I remember thinking. *Boy, she must really be dedicated to it.*

I glanced at my lawn. It seemed fine.

As the summer days rolled along, I noticed other occasions where my neighbor had her sprinkler going in full force. I'm not even sure I knew where our sprinkler was.

As the scorching 100-plus degree days of August settled in, I noticed patches of grass on our lawn that were beginning to turn yellow and die. The same thing was also happening to other lawns in our neighborhood.

The sun is just too intense for the grass, I thought.

Then I glanced at the neighbor's lawn.

No dry patches.

Same sun.

Hmmmmm.

It didn't take too long for the obvious to dawn on me. My neighbor had taken care of her lawn. She had been watering it regularly. I had not. Now, when the heat was on, her lawn stayed healthy while ours was starting to look like the landscape from an old Western movie, complete with prickly cactuses and blowing tumbleweeds.

There are two immediate parenting applications I took from my neighbor's good lawn-keeping habits that relate to our last two chapters. They have stuck with me to this day and I'd like to share them with you.

Water your lawn regularly. Imagine that your positive attention is the water and your kids are the lawn. We have talked about pointing out your kids' positive behavior and underlying positive traits, but I have not told you how often you should do this.

QUESTION: *How often should you water your lawn (if you don't want it to look like the New Mexico desert)?*

Answer: Regularly. If possible, every day.

You have dozens of opportunities each day to notice and point out your kids' positive behaviors and traits. *I recommend that you point out your kids' positive behaviors and traits between three to five times a day.* Every day. Some days you may point out fewer than three and other days you might even do more than five. No problem. But aim for at least three a day—on the good days and the bad days. In fact, I have seen many times when a parent pointing out positive behavior has even helped a child bounce back from a bad morning and end up with a good day overall.

Over time, your consistent positive encouragement will accumulate in your child's memory, just as the water from the sprinkler strengthens and nourishes the grass roots beneath the surface. Your positive and affirming words will echo in your child's mind, reminding him or her of their positive choices, the positive results of making those choices, and the positive traits that you see growing inside of them.

Water the *whole* lawn. One evening, I was showing Matt and Shelby how to effectively point out the positive behavior of their challenging eight-year-old son. As we finished our discussion, Matt and Shelby were both excited about getting started. Then a concerned look came over Matt's face.

"What about our other kids?" he asked. "Won't they feel left out?"

Matt was right. If you only water one part of the lawn, you will only have one patch of green grass. If you want the whole lawn to be green, you need to water all of it. While you may have one child who requires some extra attention for a season, make sure to look for the positive behavior and traits of *all* your kids.

When you do this, several wonderful things happen. First, each of your kids feels noticed and encouraged on a regular basis. Second, your kids get to hear you point out the positive behavior of their siblings, which reminds them that their siblings actually have positive behavior. Third, you are setting an example of making encouraging comments all your kids can follow. Finally, you are creating an environment where all your kids feel noticed, valued, and appreciated.

You will have a green, healthy lawn instead of an arid patch.

That's what a little regular watering will do.

ENCOURAGING TIP #3:
When you point out the positive behavior and traits of all your kids on a regular basis, you create an encouraging family atmosphere where good habits and strong relationships can grow.

Consider:
How does the illustration of watering the whole lawn apply to you and your family? How will pointing out each of your kids' positive behavior on a regular basis affect your family environment? What lesson does doing this teach your kids?

Chapter 29

Look Past the Failure

It was a sunny Saturday afternoon and Jake's second-grade baseball team was halfway through practice. The boys had practiced hitting, fielding, and scooping up ground balls and were now taking a short water break. Parents were scattered along the edge of the baseball diamond, some standing, others sitting on a small set of aluminum bleachers, while siblings ran around beside the field, playing assorted games of tag and catch.

"You guys want to have a scrimmage?" asked Coach Mel.

"Yeah!" came the resounding response from the team, as if this was the question they had been waiting for all practice. The coaches quickly divided the players into two relatively even teams and the scrimmage began. I can't tell you which team won the scrimmage. In fact, there is only one thing I remember about that particular scrimmage and it occurred at the very end.

When the scrimmage was over, Coach Mel summoned the players over to him so he could give them a few more pointers and encouraging words. Everyone hustled over except Derek, who had evidently been on the losing scrimmage team. That was easy to figure out because he was sitting on the grass, or to be more accurate, flailing around on the grass, throwing one of the biggest temper tantrums I had seen in recent memory.

Derek's dad went over to try to console him but was relatively unsuccessful. I could still hear Derek crying as he climbed into their family van.

This boy had a hard time looking past the failure.

Failure is tough. You might think that failure is a rather strong term for simply having lost a scrimmage game during a baseball practice. You are right. But that was how Derek was thinking about it. It was a failure. He was on the losing team. He had so badly wanted to win, but he had not been a good enough player to save the day. Maybe he had struck out or dropped a fly ball. What will the other kids think of him now? He clearly must not be one of the better players on the team. Maybe he is one of the worst. Do they even want him on the team now?

These thoughts are called negative thinking traps. They remind me of traps because you often don't recognize them when you step into them, and once you are in them, it can be tricky to free yourself. But the most dastardly part of negative thinking traps is not just that they are negative in flavor; it is that they are *not true*.

Here are two of the most common negative thinking traps that you can teach your kids to be on the lookout for:

Exaggerating the Negative—focusing on the negative parts of a situation and forgetting the positive parts of that same situation; treating a small problem as if it were much bigger than it really is.

True thoughts that will help avoid this trap: Everyone makes mistakes. I can do better next time. I made a few mistakes, but I also did some things really well. You can't win them all. Even if I lose, I will still be a good sport. I can try again. I did my best, that's all I can do. I can do better next time. Even if I lost or made a mistake, God will help me handle this the right way.

Using Extreme Words—viewing a situation in extreme terms by using words like *always, never, everyone, no one,* and so on. Examples: I always get in trouble. No one ever invites me to play. I never win. I'll always be terrible at math.

True thoughts that will help avoid this trap: I got in trouble because I made a bad choice; when I make good choices, things go much better. Everyone loses sometimes. If I want more friends, then I can join a club or try to be friendlier to others. Lots of kids get better at things if they keep on trying. If I don't have time to play today, that's okay, I will probably have time tomorrow. I wonder if there is a lesson God wants me to learn from this. If I want to get better at _____, then I can start practicing or ask for help.

I imagine these two negative thinking traps sound familiar. We all slip into them from time to time, and your kids are no exception. Here are a few situations where negative thinking traps tend to show up:

When a task is hard or time-consuming (such as homework or cleaning a room)
Losing a competition (such as a sport or a game)
Making a small mistake that others might see (such as being late, forgetting supplies, or making an error in a performance or sport/activity)

If you want your kids to learn to recognize and avoid these traps, then sit down together and introduce them to these two negative thinking traps. They will probably recognize them right away. Then see what true thoughts you can all come up with to avoid (or step out of) these traps. Give them a few scenarios (e.g., losing a game, getting some items wrong on a test, spilling a drink in the lunchroom) and have them come up with true thoughts that will help them put the situation in a proper and accurate perspective.

When your kids learn to steer clear of negative thinking traps, they will find it easier to look past the failure and see how God can teach them a lesson through it and even bring something good from it.[4] They may eventually realize that it wasn't even a failure after all.

ENCOURAGING TIP #4:
When kids learn to look past their failures,
they will learn that God can bring something
good out of any situation.

Consider:

How often do you fall into these two negative thinking traps? How often do your kids fall into them? What are some true thoughts you and your kids can learn that will help all of you avoid these traps and learn to think things that are true and positive?

Chapter 30

Look Backward Together

Freddie was a seven-year-old I had been seeing for some time due to his bad habit of arguing with his parents and throwing fits the size of Mount Rushmore. When I am working with a child on this type of behavior, I often have the parents keep track of the child's progress with a calendar. Each day, the child gets a "Respect Score," which is simply a color-coded number from one to ten. Numbers seven and higher are written in green while numbers six and lower are written in red.

When we started Freddie's calendar, he initially got a lot of reds. I do mean a lot of reds. However, with time Freddie improved and began to have many more green days than red days. In fact, he even had one good stretch where he got more than thirty greens in a row! That was impressive to be sure, but he was not a Jedi Master yet.

As was inevitable, Freddie's green streak eventually came to an end and there were times when the red days returned. One session, when Freddie was in the midst of a rather "red" week, I thought it might be a good idea for us to review his calendar from the very beginning. We sat together on the blue couch in my office and remembered how, when we first met, Freddie used to get so many reds. As we turned the calendar pages, we saw Freddie's greens slowly increase and we looked with awe on his amazing accomplishment of more than thirty greens in a row.

"I totally forgot about that," Freddie said with a smile. "I can't believe I did that."

"Do you remember how fun that was?" I asked. "You weren't arguing about homework or bedtime. If you started to get mad, you must have stopped it and turned it around. You took deep breaths and calmed down. You used your flexible thoughts. You did a great job."

"Yeah, I do remember. I earned a ton of my Legos back; I don't think I hardly ever got in trouble," Freddie responded, almost as if fondly recalling memories of a past vacation.

"You know what the best thing is?" I asked.

"What?"

"If you did it once, you can do it again. In fact, the first time is usually the hardest. The second time should be even easier. You might even be able to beat your own record!"

Freddie's eyes lit up. "Yeah, maybe I can," he said.

The fact: he did.

There is a simple truth we don't want you to overlook, and we don't want your kids to overlook it either. It is that while they have made plenty of bad choices, they have made many good choices as well. Even if your kids can be rather difficult at times, they have still quickly and respectfully done what you have asked them to do many times. They have listened respectfully to their teachers and coaches. They have shared with their siblings and friends. They have worked hard on homework. They have even gone to bed without a problem.

There is more. Your kids have also learned to do things that seemed very difficult at the time. Whether learning to read, beating a difficult level of a video game, gaining proficiency on an instrument, or perfecting a sports technique, all of these things were new and difficult at first but your kids stuck with them long enough now to feel comfortable.

If you have difficult kids, I know they haven't always done these things, and their behavior can often be very frustrating. But they have made good choices sometimes, and sometimes is much different than no times. That is what we don't want you to forget. We especially don't want them to forget it. Because if they have done it once, they can certainly do it again.

Freddie had truly forgotten about his month of greens. That is not unusual. Kids often make the mistake of remembering their mistakes and forgetting their successes. That is not good. Reminding Freddie of the good choices he had made in the past was the first step in helping him to realize he could do it again.

Many times, biblical authors take us on a journey back through history to help us remember God's faithfulness, the tragic results of disobedience, and the blessings that came when the Israelites returned to God in repentance and obedience.[5] God wants us to remember the past and learn from it. We want your kids to do the same.

Here's what you do. From time to time, sit down with your kids and reflect back on the good choices they have made, important lessons they have learned (from good and bad choices), and challenges they have overcome. You might be surprised at how few they remember. Be prepared with examples of times they have been respectful, asked for help when they were confused, acted considerately toward a sibling or peer, helped someone in need, worked hard on something, turned a bad situation around, and treated others the way God wants us to. Let them know how proud you are of them for making these choices and help them realize the positive blessings that these choices brought, both to them and to others.

The lesson is obvious: If they did it once, they can do it again.

Your kids know they have made some bad choices.

Don't let them forget the good ones.

ENCOURAGING TIP #5:
**When you help your kids remember
their good choices, it encourages them to make even more.**

Consider:

What impact will it have if you occasionally review your kids' positive choices and the good results that followed? You can also review a few negative choices and the results that followed and then let your kids compare the two. What positive and edifying lesson can they learn from this kind of discussion?

TOOL #7
CORRECTING

Chapter 31

Focus on Your Job

It was a sunny afternoon and Lora, who was very pregnant with our second son, had taken two-year-old Jake to the park for the morning. After a fun time of running, swinging, and climbing in the Ohio sunshine, she decided to cap off the morning by treating Jake to a Happy Meal and a bit of inside playtime at a nearby McDonald's Playland. It didn't take Jake long to down a few French fries and most of a cheeseburger and then he was off to play in the ball pit, climb up the colorful tubes, slide down, and then do it all over and over again.

When it was time to pack up and head home, Lora discovered that Jake had found a comfortable spot in a multicolored compartment at the very top of a tube. He was just sitting there contently, apparently enjoying the view. Lora called for him to come down and he just looked at her. Then he looked away.

Uh-oh.

She called again and he didn't budge. And again. And again. Still no budge. So with no other options in sight and in all of her pregnant glory, Lora hefted herself into the ball pit, squeezed into the colored tube, and slowly crawled up to the top on her hands and knees, as her son looked on in wide-eyed disbelief. Once she had him securely in her arms, she maneuvered to the slide and enjoyed the return trip back to ground level, to the applause of the other McDonald's Playland moms.

Apparently, Jake had a lesson to learn about listening to his mom and it was our job to teach it to him.

I was recently talking to Cynthia, a mom in my office, who was extremely concerned about her eleven-year-old son's oppositional behavior. However, she was equally concerned about her own angry responses, which she knew were not helping the situation any. "I have read every parenting book you can name," she told me. "But nothing is working and I know that the way my husband and I handle things sometimes just makes it worse."

Like many of us, Cynthia and her husband were getting sidetracked by their own mad thoughts, which were just making things worse.

"Why are they arguing again?"

"Why doesn't she just listen for once?"

"I can't believe he is talking to me that way!"

"This is ridiculous!"

"I've had it with her nonsense!"

It takes all of one second for these thoughts to captivate your brain and emotions. When they do, your anger takes over and your parenting effectiveness takes a nosedive. Why? Because you are forgetting one main thing: to focus on your job. What is your job when correction is needed? To teach your kids the right lesson, the right way.

In Galatians 5:22–23, Paul lists the fruit of the Spirit, which include love, joy, peace, patience, kindness, goodness, faithfulness, gentleness, and self-control. These characteristics are not just intended for our easy parenting days but for the difficult ones as well. So how do you keep mad thoughts from taking over your brain so you can respond to your kids' negative behavior with wisdom and a spirit of gentleness and self-control?

You remember what your job is. You need to fill your head with parent flexible thoughts, designed to help you stay calm and focused in difficult situations.

> The calmer I am the more effective teacher I will be.
>
> I want Anna to follow my example, instead of me following hers.
>
> God has put me here to show my kids how to handle things the right way and that's what I'm going to do.
>
> What is the lesson Maggie needs to learn right now? What is the best way to help her learn it?
>
> Lord, help me handle this situation in a way that builds my family, not in a way that tears it down.
>
> Evan is out of control right now; I need to stay in control.

Choose three of these and memorize them. When your kids misbehave, flood your mind with these thoughts that help you stay focused on the job God has given you to do. You will stay in control. You will talk calmly and respectfully. You will think of more effective negative consequences. You will be too busy being an effective teacher to waste time losing your cool.

Because you are staying focused on one thing: doing your job.

Lora brought Jake home from McDonald's and we focused on our job of helping him learn the right lesson. First, he went right to time-out. Next, we decided that he would not be going back to McDonald's Playland anytime soon because of his choice to ignore his mom. Then, about a month later, he and I went to McDonald's a few times only to practice going to the top of the tube and immediately coming down at my request. Once he had done this successfully several times to show he had learned his lesson, *then* we could go to McDonald's to play again.

When you stay focused on doing your job, you will handle difficult parenting situations more effectively. You will build your family up instead of tearing it down. And your kids will learn the right lessons, the right way.

CORRECTING TIP #1:
Using parent flexible thoughts will help you focus
on your job, stay in control of your emotions,
and teach the right lessons, the right way.

Consider:
What parenting situations frustrate you the most? Name three flexible thoughts that will help you stay focused on your job in those situations.

Chapter 32

Help Your Kids Bounce

Picture a basketball with too little air in it. You drop it on the gymnasium floor and instead of bouncing, it lands with a plop. The NBA players won't want this ball. The college hoopsters won't use this ball. Even the kids on the elementary playground will leave this ball behind and choose another.

Everyone wants a ball that bounces.

Your kids will have many good days, but if they are normal at all, they will have their share of bad ones as well. What do we want your kids to do after they have a bad day?

Have another one?

No.

We want them to bounce.

We want them to bounce back to respectful behavior as quickly as possible, rather than get stuck in their disrespectful behavior, like a basketball that has no air. Bouncing back is an important life skill, and you can help your kids learn to do it.

Camila was a seven-year-old girl who didn't bounce very well.

When she got mad, she often stayed mad. And then she got mad about something else. Sandra, Camila's mom, could tell when it was going to be a bad day. She told me she could just see that look in Camila's eyes.

She was usually right.

I spent a lot of time working with Camila on how to think *after* she had made a bad choice, or *after* she had a bad day. Because the way she thinks *at the end of* a bad day now becomes the way she is thinking *before* the next day. And we want her to think in a way that will help her bounce.

So when you are talking with your kids at the end of a rough day, after a time-out, or at the end of any negative situation, use words that will help them get moving in a positive direction. Help them see that their negative choices are now over and the goal is to learn a good lesson from their bad choices and get back to their good choices.

In other words, they can bounce.

"Well, today was a bit of a sad day and you had to go to bed early, but you learned some important lessons. I'm proud of you for that. So now tomorrow can be a great day."

"What is the main lesson you learned from today that can help you have a great day tomorrow?"

"We've had one time-out today, but you learned a good lesson about how important it is to use your words in a nice way. So now we can use that lesson to help us have a great day and use our words in a friendly way."

You can even help your kids bounce by the way you tell them no. When kids hear the word no, it is similar to a door being shut in their face. With their momentary limited perspective, all they can see is the closed door, which they immediately try to pound on to reopen.

Example:

Nick: "Mom, can I play a computer game?" (hoping the door will open)

Mom: "No, not today." (slams the door shut)

Nick: "Why not? You never let me play! It's not fair!" (pounding on the door, trying to get it to open)

Instead, you can tell your kids no in a way that will help them see other doors that are not so bad, will work just as well, or may even be better.

Example:

Nick: "Mom, can I play a computer game?" (hoping the door will open)

Mom: "It is too close to bedtime for that right now, pal, but you can probably play a computer game tomorrow after school." (gently closes the door but points to another door)

Or

Nick: "Mom, can I play a computer game?" (hoping the door will open)

Mom: "Well, your sister is using the computer right now, but I'm sure you can play on it later this afternoon. Maybe you and I can find something fun to do right now." (gently closes one door but points to another)

Notice that the word "no" was not even used in the two examples above. In each example, a simple reason was given why Nick could not play on the computer right now and then the mother redirected his attention to another positive alternative.

She chose words that would help Nick bounce.

If you help your kids see the next positive step that they can take, they are a bit more likely to take it. The fact is that many times they don't see that next positive step on their own. They need your help. At times, they will still not bounce, even with all of your wonderful assistance, but then you can help them bounce back from that too.

With practice and perseverance, they can be like a basketball filled with air.

Everyone wants to play with that ball.

CORRECTING TIP #2:
Your choice of words can help your kids bounce back from a bad day or difficult situation.

Consider:
Do your kids tend to get stuck instead of bouncing back from a bad moment or a bad day? What can you say to your kids after a negative moment that will help them bounce back more quickly?

Chapter 33

Make a Quick Response

Sitting in my office during our very first meeting one wintery Tuesday evening, Amy began giving me an example of her son's oppositional behavior, which I was told had been going on for years.

"Kyle was downstairs playing a video game," she began. "I called down to him and told him to come up and start his reading. Fifteen minutes later, he's still down there. He hasn't moved an inch!"

Whoops.

I have seen a lot of oppositional kids and teens over the past twenty years and have noticed a few things that the parents of those kids often have in common. Not always, but often. One of those is a slow response time.

In Amy's situation, she had asked Kyle to stop his video game and come upstairs. Fifteen minutes later he had not responded and was still playing. That is when Amy got frustrated and yelled at Kyle for the second time to get moving.

Her response was about fourteen minutes and forty-five seconds too slow, causing several problems:

Kyle knew his mom had asked him to turn the game off.

Kyle knew that he had not answered her and that this was disrespectful.

Kyle's disrespectful choice earned him an extra fourteen minutes of video game time.

Kyle is likely to do it again because it paid off.

Kyle is learning to be disrespectful.

Without realizing it, Amy is the one who is teaching him.

Here is an important question: When you ask your kids to do something (or to stop doing something), what do you want them to *say* and *do*? Here is how I would answer that question:

Say. Within five seconds or so, reply with a respectful verbal response. This could include saying "Okay," asking a reasonable question, or making a reasonable comment related to your request. Any of these is fine, although the most common should be just saying, "Okay." The key is that the verbal response happens right away and is said in a respectful way.

Do. Unless you decide otherwise because of your child's question or comment, you want your child to do the thing you asked right away. Remember, inherent in most parental requests is the word "now." You usually do not say, "Kyle, please go brush your teeth *now*"; instead you just say, "Kyle, please go brush your teeth." But now is implied, and your child knows it. If you say, "Please brush your teeth when the TV show is over," then you have indicated a different time frame and that is just fine.

It is very helpful to have a clear idea (as outlined above) of what you expect your kids to say and do when you make a parental request. When they do it, you can give them a squeeze on the shoulder and point out that they were very respectful, helpful, polite, and so on.

However, if they don't respond in a respectful way, you need to react quickly.

Within about five to ten seconds. Not joking. Your reaction should be one of two things, depending on your child's response.

Help them make a U-turn. This simply means that you will encourage them to respond quickly and respectfully as discussed above. Here's how it would sound:

Amy: "Kyle, time to turn the game off and come upstairs to do your reading."

Kyle: No response.

Amy: (calmly, after five to ten seconds) "Kyle, I said it's time to stop playing now. Pal, it's important that you answer right away when I talk to you, do you understand?"

Kyle: "Yep, sorry."

Amy: "Okay. Let's try again. I would like you to turn off the game and do your reading."

Kyle: "Okay, I'm coming."

Make sure your child learns the right lesson from a negative choice. If your child continues to ignore you, talks back, argues, or is unresponsive to your attempt to help him make a U-turn, then you can decide what negative consequence will best suit the situation and inform him of your decision. For example, if Kyle argues about stopping a video game, then video game privileges can be discontinued for the rest of that day and the next. Or more.

One final note. You will find that when you respond quickly to your child's negative behavior, the quality and effectiveness of your response will greatly improve. You will be calmer and better able to communicate in an effective and respectful way. After all, you have been frustrated for all of five to ten seconds, so you haven't even hit "super" frustrated mode yet. Either way, it is much better than trying to stay calm when you have been frustrated for the past fourteen minutes and forty-five seconds, as Amy had discovered.

The good news is that Amy learned to respond quickly and calmly to Kyle's negative choices. As a result, Kyle learned that listening to her the first time was a very good idea. Much better than the alternative. Your kids can learn that too.

A quick response will help make it happen.

CORRECTING TIP #3:
A quick response will help your kids
learn that negative choices get them nowhere. Fast.

Consider:

Why is a quick response better than a slow response when your child misbehaves? How will a quick response improve your effectiveness in teaching your kids the right lesson the right way?

Chapter 34

Teach the Right Lesson

Nate was an eight-year-old boy sitting in my office, looking like he would rather be anywhere else. His parents were also there and were giving me an update on Nate's behavior. Kim, Nate's mother, began to describe one recent instance where Nate had taken a long time to put down the iPad and start his homework, despite her repeated requests. As a result of ignoring his mother, Nate had lost iPad privileges for a few days.

"It's not fair!" Nate injected, frustrated. "I just needed a few more minutes to finish what I was doing. She just kept bothering me and wouldn't leave me alone."

Nate obviously had several lessons to learn, not the least of which included listening to his mother and speaking more respectfully. And really, that's what discipline is: helping your kids learn an important lesson from a bad choice they have made.

There are many times when a negative consequence is needed to help them learn that lesson. You can choose from many negative consequences, including privilege loss, time-out, early bedtime, assigning additional chores, practicing positive behavior, and writing flexible sentences.[1] However, in this chapter, I want to remind you of the main lesson all of these consequences are designed to teach.

It is a lesson Nate desperately needed to learn.

Simply put, we want our kids to learn that respectful behavior always is the best choice. There is always a respectful way to handle a situation and a good solution for any problem. If your kids can't think of it, you will be happy to help them figure it out. On the flip side, there is virtually never a time when it is okay to be hurtful or disrespectful to others with our words or actions. The problem is that kids keep forgetting this lesson. Negative consequences are designed to help them remember it.

Nate's comments indicated that he failed to see the connection between his behavior and the consequence his mother had given him (losing iPad privileges). I have found a simple way to explain the connection between respectful behavior and privileges to kids. I call it "The Lesson of the Circles." I taught it to Nate that session and you can easily show it to your kids.

Someday, they may even thank you for it.

THE LESSON OF THE CIRCLES

Sit down with your kids and with your left hand, make a circle with your thumb and first finger, like you are making an "okay" sign. This circle represents your kids' respectful behavior. They can be more respectful (raise your hand higher) or less respectful (lower your hand). Ask your kids who is in charge of this circle. The answer is that they are. Only they control their choice to be respectful or disrespectful. Only they make the circle go up or down.

Now make a circle with your thumb and first finger on your right hand. This is the "fun" circle. It represents your kids' privileges or fun. Again, it can go up (raise your hand) or down (lower your hand). Ask your kids who controls their fun circle, or their privileges. A lot of kids answer this one incorrectly. The answer is that you do. This may momentarily shock them. But the fact is that Mom and Dad control all of the fun privileges they have. Television, toys, video games, bicycles, playing with friends—Mom and Dad are in charge of all of these. They can allow the kids to have them or remove them at any time.

Now comes the lesson part.

Because you love your kids so much, there are many important lessons you want them to learn. One of those lessons is that it is important to treat others the way God wants us to. To treat them with value, love, and respect (raise your left circle). One of the ways you will teach your kids to do that is by treating them that way and by treating others that way as well.

However, another way is to take the fun circle and hook it (take your right circle and connect it to the left circle) to the respect circle. That way, when your kids take their respect circle high by treating others respectfully (e.g., listening to parents, good effort at school, respectful to siblings), their fun circle goes high too (raise the left circle which will also raise the right circle). However, if they choose to treat others disrespectfully (lower the left circle which will also lower the right circle), then their privileges will go down accordingly. In fact, there is no way for the fun circle to go up unless the respect circle goes up first.

The two circles are always hooked.

That is why Nate's iPad privileges were taken away. His respect circle went down (due to ignoring his mom) and so did his fun circle.

And there is only one way for his fun circle to go back up: His respect circle will need to go up first.

That is the lesson of the circles.

Teach it to your kids today.

CORRECTING TIP #4:
**The only way to make the
fun circle go up is making the respect circle go up first.**

Consider:
What do you think of the lesson of the circles? Is this a lesson your kids need to learn? How can you make sure that they experience this lesson in real life?

Chapter 35

Teach the Right Lesson the Right Way

Yelling. An angry, intimidating look. A harsh tone. Put-downs and critical comments. Slapping or hitting in anger. Grabbing a child by the arm more tightly than you have to. I know parents who have done each of these. All are ineffective and inappropriate. Some of them can even be verbally or physically abusive.

None of them help you be an effective teacher.

Anyone who has been a parent for more than a week will tell you that challenging child behavior can quickly elicit impulsive, angry responses from even the most calm and mild-mannered of us. I am a fairly even-tempered guy, and I remember a few times marveling at the level of anger my young boys' behavior would occasionally cause to swell up inside me. I am embarrassed to say that it was usually because I was busy doing something else and their behavior was interrupting my progress. Likewise, I have had many loving parents tell me that they are not always proud of how they have handled correction moments.

Join the club.

Two elements are part of every correction situation: content and style. In the last chapter, we discussed the content, or the lesson you want your kids to learn. In this chapter, we will talk about your style.

The Bible clearly instructs us to discipline and train our children.[2] But we would do well to also remember that Jesus commands us to treat others the way we would like to be treated[3] (e.g., correct others the way we would like to be corrected if we were in their shoes), while Proverbs encourages us to seek and act with wisdom[4] and the apostle Paul tells us to treat others with patience, gentleness, and self-control.[5]

In other words, the Bible says that your style is a big deal.

Your kids would tend to agree.

I can recall sixteen-year-old Robby who wanted nothing to do with his father anymore because of years of a critical correction style. Ten-year-old Morgan comes to mind, who had a close relationship with her father (he was firm but warm) but was distant from her mother due to her mother's demanding, short-tempered style. Eighteen-year-old Lauren loved her dad but was hesitant to talk with him about difficult subjects due to his angry, occasionally obscenity-laced responses.

I could go on.

Picture yourself on one side of a deep valley and your kids on the other side. A bridge crosses the valley. There is a lot of wisdom, guidance, and experience you want to get from your side of the bridge over to your kids. The only way for all of that valuable cargo to get from your side over to your kids is for it to cross the bridge. If it doesn't go over the bridge, it doesn't go over at all.

The bridge is your communication style. Ironically, your communication style is both most important and most at risk in correction moments. Isn't that interesting? The time when your kids need your teaching and guidance the most is when you are at the greatest risk of buggering the whole thing up.

You can basically choose one of two styles.

> One that opens your kids up to what you have to say or one that shuts them down.
> One that draws them closer to you or one that pushes them away.
> One that builds your bridge stronger or one that damages it, like dropping grenades on it.
> One that causes your kids to say, "Open the gate, Dad is coming! Mom is coming!" or one that causes them to say, "Close the gate, Dad is coming! Mom is coming!"

Take a moment and reflect on your correction style. Where is it strong and where does it need to improve? If you are like most of us, you may have a little of both.

Think about what an effective correction style would look like. Parents with an effective correction style will be frustrated at times, to be sure. But they will be in control. They will follow the Family Respect Rule. They will stay focused on the goal: To teach the kids the right lesson, the right way. By the "right way," I mean they will teach their lessons in a way that strengthens their relationships, rather than damages them. Even when privileges are removed, they will do it in a controlled and respectful way—a way that teaches a lesson without misusing their power and position as a parent. The parents will leave their kids feeling lucky that they have them for a mom or dad.

Do you want to get your message across to your kids? Do you want to correct your kids in an effective way? Use a style that will communicate that you love them and want them to learn an important lesson that will always be beneficial. Correct them out of love and concern, not anger.

Use a style that will cause them to open the gate for you.

CORRECTING TIP #5:
**Your correction style will open your kids
up or shut them down to the lessons God wants
them to learn from you.**

Consider:
Why do you think a parent's correction style is so important? Is there anything about your style that could damage the bridge? What changes do you need to make to protect and even build your communication bridge?

TOOL #8
LEADING

Chapter 36

Remember the Power of Your Example

"Where on earth did he hear that word?" Tony and Donna asked in shocked disbelief after being told about a few choice words that Carson, their second-grade son, had used during recess. Unfortunately for Carson, he had been within earshot of the recess monitor, who relayed the boy's newfound vocabulary to his teacher, who decided to pass the information along to his parents.

Carson's new word was not likely to be on a spelling bee anytime soon.

Tony and Donna immediately started scouring their collective memories. After all, words like that don't just pop out of nowhere. It would be inappropriate if a sixteen-year-old used that word, let alone their seven-year-old. Could it be something he heard on TV? From his older brother? Maybe he heard it from another kid at school.

I have known many parents who are understandably vigilant about what their kids could be exposed to through television, computers, movies, video games, music, and other kids. They are right to be careful about these powerful influencers and proceed with caution. However, I find it ironic that many parents worry about television's influence and at the same time seem almost totally oblivious to a far greater influence on their kids' behavior that is right in front of their noses. Or should I say right behind their noses.

Themselves.

Kids do learn from watching. And during the formative eighteen years or so they live at home, there is one thing they will watch more often and with more repetition and with more intensity than any other single thing: you. You are like a television show that is always on, no commercial breaks, no fast-forwarding. Your kids see the good and the bad. The shining moments and the moments you would like to take back. They have seen your good side and your ugly side. They have likely seen the real you more often than your best friend or coworkers have. And before they leave home to venture out into life as a young adult, they will have seen it thousands of times.

And you're concerned about television.

Ever wondered why a piano teacher doesn't give lessons over the phone? Sounds ludicrous, doesn't it? In order to be effective, a piano teacher must be able to watch her students, but then she also wants them to be able to watch her as she demonstrates how to play with proper technique. There is no better way to learn. This is one of the reasons YouTube has become so popular. In a matter of seconds, you can find a tutorial for how to do almost anything—a tutorial that you can watch and listen to over and over again. I suspect the apostle Paul was well aware of the power of example when he invited the believers in Corinth to "follow my example, as I follow the example of Christ."[1]

The power of your example is not something to be feared, unless you are frequently misusing it. The power of the piano teacher's example is only a problem if she shows her students how to play incorrectly. Conversely, it is a wonderful teaching tool if she shows them how to play correctly. In fact, the power of example reflects the way God designed people to learn and families to work. You can lead your kids by looking for opportunities to use your example to show them how to think flexibly and accurately, speak intelligently and respectfully, and treat others with grace and kindness.

I didn't say to just tell them how to do these things.

You show them how.

For example, the other day while I was working at the computer, Lora was facing a stack of laundry that was almost as tall as she. I heard her say, "There is *sooo* much laundry to do," but then, rather than following up that phrase with a complaint, she caught herself and said, "but laundry means that I have a family to take care of and I'm very thankful for that."

You have to admit, that's a pretty good example.

Two weeks ago in my office, I was involved in a discussion with Caden, a teenager, and his father. During the session, I was happy to be able to pause the discussion and point out to the boy that even though his dad was concerned and upset about Caden's frequently disrespectful style of talking to his parents, his dad had remained calm and had listened really well to his son throughout the session, which made it a much easier and more productive conversation.

That's a pretty good example too.

When you are aware of the power of your example, you can use that example to show your kids how to do many things:

Encourage others
Speak respectfully
Listen to understand
Use flexible thoughts
Treat others with warmth and kindness

Your kids will spend more hours watching you than they will ever watch TV. You are right to be thoughtful about what shows and channels they watch. Be thoughtful and intentional about what they see on your channel as well.

LEADING TIP #1:
Kids learn by watching, and your example
is the thing they will watch the most.

Consider:
How was your life influenced by your parents' example when you were a child? How much of an influence do you think a parent's example has on a child? What is one area your child needs to improve in and how can you use your example as one part of the learning process?

Chapter 37

Practice Your Faith with Your Kids

Every now and then I run across the term "practical atheist." This term is used to describe a person who says he believes in God but lives his life as if God were not real. I know there are times in my life when this has been true of me. The pull of this world, the busyness of life, and my own sinful tendencies dull my mind and, like the proverbial frog in the kettle, I find myself gradually moving through my daily life as though God were not real or relevant.

As His own children He is shaping into His image and as leaders in our homes, God does not want us to be professing Christians but practical atheists. In Deuteronomy 6:5–9, Moses tells the children of Israel:

> Love the Lord your God will all your heart and with all your soul and with all your strength. These commandments that I give you today are to be on your hearts. Impress them on your children. Talk about them when you sit at home and when you walk along

the road, when you lie down and when you get up. Tie them as symbols on your hands and bind them on your foreheads. Write them on the doorframes of your houses and on your gates.

The message is clear: God wants us to practice our faith and weave it into every part of our lives. He wants us to continually live our faith alongside our kids and with our kids, so they get a real picture of what a genuine Christian life is supposed to look like. Without that, learning to be a Christian is like trying to put together a jigsaw puzzle without the box-top picture to look at. That is a difficult thing to do. God has given your kids a picture to look at and that picture is you. In fact, not only are you the picture, you are going to show them how to put the puzzle together by doing it with them.

In a very real sense, this entire book has been about how to live out your faith with your kids in a real way. None of us will do it perfectly as we'll see, but we can all do it genuinely. If you are a grandparent or an aunt or uncle who sees a child frequently, the same is true for you. If you are aware that your box-top picture has been sending the wrong message to your kids, there is no time like the present to start sending the right one. If you realize that your box-top has not been guiding your kids toward a stronger Christian faith because you have never established your own personal relationship with God, then I encourage you to surrender your life to God even now, begin reading the Bible (the gospel of Mark is a good place to start), and talk to a local pastor about taking the first steps in your new Christian journey.

Here are four simple ways you can practice your Christian faith in a way that will help your kids experience God's reality as a very real part of their daily lives.

Weave discussion about God into daily life. Life brings no short-age of situations in which to apply God's promises and biblical prin-ciples. Peter tells us to "cast all your anxiety on him because he cares for you."[2] Whether it is giving thanks for everyday blessings, thinking together as a family about how God wants us to treat each other, or talking together about life events in a way that reflects a desire to seek God's guidance (e.g., moving, switching schools, handling peer prob-lems, helping those in need), you will help your kids put their faith into practice when you tackle life's everyday issues together by acknowledg-ing God's presence and seeking His wisdom.

Read together. This can take many forms, depending on your kids' ages. Over the years, Jake, Luke, and I have read and discussed several age-appropriate books on Christian living (for students/teens), dating, and apologetics, to name a few subjects, and Lora and I often read books on marriage together. Of course, family times are a great time to read and discuss short passages from Scripture, devotional books, or books for children, teens, or families. Reading together gives you thoughtful and intelligent (perhaps even challenging) content to reflect on together, which can strengthen your relationships and shape the way your kids think about the truth behind God's principles and commands and how it can impact their everyday lives.

Serve together. Serving others can take many forms. It may in-clude volunteering at a local food shelter, serving at your local church, packaging food that will be sent to families in need in poverty-stricken countries, supporting and praying for a child from a third-world coun-try, or going on a mission trip. However you are able to, serving with your kids is a wonderful way to help them learn firsthand that there are others with great needs and that God wants us to use our resources—our time, money, and talents—to help meet those needs. As James reminds us, "Religion that God our Father accepts as pure and faultless is this: to look after orphans and widows in their distress and to keep oneself from being polluted by the world."[3]

Pray together. Growing up, bedtimes and family times gave us many regular opportunities to pray with and for each other. As our boys have moved into their early twenties, the opportunities for praying together are not as frequent, which means I need to be on the lookout and even create a few of my own. For example, Luke has been dating a wonderful girl for the past couple of months, and he and I recently took a few minutes to pray together that God would bless their friendship and give them both wisdom as He guides their lives. No matter your child's age, praying together is a powerful way of bringing life's joys, pains, and thanksgiving to a loving and caring God—and doing it with your kids.

There is simply no fooling your kids. Nor would you want to. If your faith is genuine, your kids will know it. Ask yourself if you are practicing your faith with your kids in the midst of everyday circumstances. Are you living like a practical atheist or like a practicing Christian?

LEADING #2:
When you live your faith with your kids, you are writing God's commands on the doorframes of their hearts.

Consider:
Why do you think it is important to "live your faith" with your kids? What is one way you can live your faith with your kids and family in the areas of daily conversation, reading, serving, and praying?

Chapter 38

Do Right Right

Ed sat in my office and described the angry, disrespectful behavior of his thirteen-year-old daughter, Samantha. When seemingly reasonable requests were made of her, Samantha often ignored them, responded sarcastically, and had even thrown things in a fit of anger. This behavior had been going on for some time and was now hitting a critical point where something needed to change.

As Ed described Samantha's behavior, something struck me about the way he spoke that was different from many other dads I have talked with. Rather than being perplexed, frustrated, and concerned about his daughter's negative behavior, Ed was irritated by it. When I hinted at exploring the quality of family relationships, Ed was clearly not interested. In fact, this dad did not believe there was anything he needed to change at all. He wanted me to change his daughter's behavior or to tell him how to do it. Nothing more.

As you might imagine, there was more to the story. When I spoke with Samantha, I discovered that she and her father were not very close and had not been for several years. I also noticed that Samantha immediately downplayed her own negative behavior and focused almost exclusively on her dad's bad temper.

Just as her dad had done about her.

I have met a few parents (both moms and dads) like Ed with sons or daughters who were behaving like Samantha. The parents wanted their kids to walk down one path while they led the way down another. I can remember marveling once at another mom whose fourth-grade boy had gotten in trouble for swearing at school.

"Has he heard any words like that around the house?" I asked.

"Well, yeah, we swear sometimes," the mother replied sheepishly, "but he knows he's not supposed to."

Uh-huh.

Here's an exercise I'd like you to do. Think about three specific behaviors you would like your kids to improve at. The options are virtually endless. For example:

> Help with household chores in a friendly way
> Talk more respectfully
> Solve problems productively
> Bounce back from disappointment
> Be more flexible when things don't go their way
> Take turns and share more often
> Be a good sport (win or lose)
> Do their best on schoolwork

Now ask yourself this question: *Am I showing those behaviors consistently myself?* Avoid the temptation to quickly and assuredly answer yes and move on to the next chapter. Really think about it. Many of us will find that, especially on the task-oriented items such as working hard or putting our things away, we may be doing pretty well. It is often the relationship-oriented items that can be a different story.

For example, if you want your kids to speak respectfully, are you speaking respectfully to them? Do you speak respectfully to your spouse—even when you are frustrated or angry? Are you watching your own volume level and tone and working to be an easy-to-listen-to parent, husband, or wife? If you want your kids to listen and thoughtfully respond when people speak to them, are you a good listener? Do you take the time to listen to understand and let them really empty their dump truck? When you lose a game, do you model flexible thinking and act like a good sport or do you act like a sore loser and then try to disguise it by calling it being competitive? Do you use regular family times as an opportunity to build a sense of family closeness and talk through issues together in a respectful way?

We've talked about the power of our example. Right now, I want you to fine-tune your focus and think about the example you are setting with regard to the specific behaviors you want your kids to improve on. Respectful communication. Doing things for others. Being open to constructive feedback.

I encourage you to find three of these areas and make them a topic of prayer and focus this week. Determine to show your kids how to do them right. If you can't (or won't) do them right, how can you ask your kids? To take it a step further, how can you expect them to do those behaviors right if you are consistently doing them wrong? Thankfully, you can do them right and God has promised to help you do so, even if you need to seek help along the way. As you do these behaviors right, it will make it easier for your kids to do them right too.

In other words, if you want your kids to do them right, you do them right first.

LEADING TIP #3:
When your kids see you handle situations the right way, it makes it easier for them to do the same.

Consider:

How important do you think it is to show your kids how to do things right instead of just telling them? List a couple of behaviors that you want your kids to improve at (e.g., expressing frustration respectfully, being flexible, listening before talking) and then rate yourself in those same areas. What do you need to change in order to show your kids how to do right right?

Chapter 39

Do Wrong Right

Mom, can I stay outside a bit longer? Pleeeeeease?" Nine-year-old Kaitlyn was having so much fun on her backyard swing set that she couldn't bear the thought of leaving it to start the dreary task of Wednesday night fourth-grade homework.

"Sorry, sweetie," Josie replied. "It's time to come in now and get started on homework."

Not the answer Kaitlyn was hoping for.

"Mom, I don't want to come in now. Just let me play a little bit longer!" Kaitlyn had now begun arguing.

"Kaitlyn, I said it is time to come in now. You've been playing for half an hour," Josie replied firmly.

"Noooo, I don't want to," came Kaitlyn's response. "Why can't I play a bit more? You never let me!"

Josie was not in the mood for another drawn-out argument. "Listen," she shouted, "you get in here right now or you will not be out here again for the rest of the week!" Instantly, Josie realized her anger was starting to get the best of her.

"Why? I don't want to!" Kaitlyn shouted back with a sulking, stub-born tone.

"Because I said so, that's why! Now get in here right now!" Josie hollered. As she heard herself make that statement, she couldn't believe her ears. The whole day had gone perfectly until now. Why was it self-destructing? Why was she starting to lose it?

Kaitlyn had somehow come to her senses and was trudging toward the house, taking small, reluctant steps, poking along on purpose. That infuriated her mother even more.

"Young lady, you had better get moving or you will be in your room for the rest of the night!" Josie said with the most intense and angry voice she could muster, as if that would help speed up Kaitlyn's gait. It didn't. Kaitlyn just continued to walk slowly toward the house with a scowl on her face and her gaze directed downward. As she reached the back porch steps, Josie grabbed her by the upper arm and escorted her quickly through the back door.

"I can't believe you did that!" Josie said, not realizing that she was actually yelling. "How can you be so selfish? Don't you think other people have things to do too? Now sit down and start your homework and I don't want to hear another word out of you!"

Here's the thing. Josie is a good mom. She loves her kids and usu-ally does a pretty good job of handling situations in a constructive way. But she knows very well that she is not a perfect parent. Neither are you and neither am I. The fact that we are not perfect parents comes as no surprise to either God or our kids. After all, God knows us inside and out, and our kids live with us every day. In the last chapter, we talked about doing right right. Our kids need us to do wrong right too. Here's how you do it:

Take responsibility for your actions. If I respond poorly in a situation, it is not my boys' fault, even if their negative behavior was the trigger for my frustration. I am in charge of how I think, what I say, and what I do. I teach this to kids in my office every day; I must say the same thing to myself.

Apologize. If, in my anger, I have spoken or acted in a way that was disrespectful or has hurt my relationship with my boys (i.e., broken the Family Respect Rule, damaged the bridge), then I am truly sorry. As best as I can, I *never* want to break the Family Respect Rule or damage the bridge between us. It is my job to apologize without giving in to the temptation to subtly blame them for my behavior.

For example, later that night, Josie could say, "Kaitlyn, I was very frustrated with how you acted when I asked you to come in. But even when I'm mad, I always want to talk to you in a respectful way. I don't think I did. I let my anger get the best of me. I'm sorry that I shouted at you and called you selfish. That shows you how we can say things we don't mean when we're angry. Sweetie, you are not a selfish girl. Even if I am frustrated with you or have to give you a consequence to help you learn an important lesson, I want to do it in a respectful way, because I love you. Okay?"

Work hard to do it better next time. I have apologized to my boys a time or two for how I handled a situation. There is nothing like a few apologies to make you conscious of an area that you need to work on. Confessing your sins to God, making them a matter of prayer, memorizing key parent flexible thoughts, sharing your challenges honestly with your spouse or accountability partner, or talking to a pastor or therapist (or all of the above) are all appropriate responses. Show your kids that you are serious by taking appropriate action to make the changes you need to make.

The Bible tells us that if we claim to be without sin, we are simply deceiving ourselves. But it goes on to tell us that if we confess our sins, God is faithful and will forgive us and purify us from all unrighteousness.[4] One of the best leadership lessons you can give your kids is not just to do right right, but to do wrong right too.

LEADING TIP #4:
Showing your kids how to do wrong right
is one of the most important lessons they will ever learn.

Consider:

Honesty time. How well do you respond when you make a poor choice at home? Do you tend to shift the blame to others, or take responsibility for your own words and actions? Why do you think it is so important for your kids to see you do wrong right?

Chapter 40

Be a Personhood Leader

I f you are a parent, you are a leader. Welcome to the club. However, let's be honest. Just because you have become a leader in your family, it doesn't mean you will be a good one.

But you want to be a good one.

So did Dale and Trish. They had three young kids and wanted to lead them the right way. Dale's father had been an alcoholic and had not set a good example for how to lead a family. Trish also wanted to have a positive leadership influence on their kids as a mom, but wasn't sure how to go about it.

God has called both of them to lead their kids "in the way they should go."[5] No matter what your family constellation is (e.g., married, single parent, remarried, grandparent), God has called you to be a leader to the children who are under your influence. In today's world of rapidly shifting morals and boundaries, these children desperately need your leadership and guidance to understand the truth of God's Word and learn to apply it to their daily lives.

In his book *Developing the Leader Within You*,[6] John Maxwell outlines five levels of leadership. At the bottom rung of the ladder is the positional leader. This level of leadership automatically applies to each of us as parents. You have leadership power simply by virtue of your position and title of parent. However, before you get too content with this level of leadership, remember that every person with a title is a *positional leader*. A teacher, band director, coach, work supervisor, even a prison warden—these are all positional leaders. People may have to follow them. That doesn't necessarily mean they want to.

In high school, I played the snare drum in concert and marching band for one year. Unfortunately, my main memories of our band director, Mr. Douglas, are of him being stern and angry. I remember watching one practice as he literally shouted at the flute and clarinet players (usually in the front row) until some of them started to cry. I think that was the point when I decided that I no longer wanted to be in the band. When I didn't sign up again the next semester, he had me called into the school counselor's office and shouted at me too. I knew I had made the right choice.

As the band director, Mr. Douglas was a positional leader. However, I didn't want to follow him. By contrast, I have had many middle-school and high-school students tell me how much they love their choir and band directors and how much they enjoy participating in those activities. In the eyes of these students, those choir and band directors have moved to the highest rung on the leadership ladder: They have become *personhood leaders*.

A personhood leader is one who people follow simply because of the way they live and interact with others. They may not even have an official leadership title. There is just something about them that makes people want to follow them. They have a spark and an integrity that attracts others and makes them want to walk along the same path.

Every parent is a positional leader. Not every parent is a personhood leader.

You can be both.

How do you become a personhood leader?

Connect. If you want your kids to want to follow you, you must establish a strong and vibrant relationship connection first. As we talked about in Tool #4, Connecting, your kids need to know how much you love and value them. Using time, touch, getting into their world, learning together, and regular family times, connecting is the first step toward becoming a personhood leader.

Inspire. Close your eyes and imagine what you would like your family to be like. When our boys were younger, I did this very exercise. I remember determining that I wanted us to be a family that was close, who treated each other respectfully, had fun together, and grew in our faith together. As we began our regular family times, I shared these goals with our family and we talked about them, adding others to the list. Everyone agreed that they sounded good, so we set out on the journey of becoming that kind of family. It is up to you (and your spouse) to determine the vision you have for your family and communicate it in a way that gets your kids excited about becoming that kind of family.

Live. The final step in becoming a personhood leader is to live out the vision you have shared with your family. This book has covered eight tools that you can use:

Talking

Listening

Influencing

Connecting

Teaching

Encouraging

Correcting

Leading

If your kids see you doing these things every day, they will see a living example of what the Christian faith looks like. They will experience a mom and dad who love them and treat them with patience, gentleness, and respect. They will learn about a God who created them, loves them, and has great and eternally significant plans for them. They will learn important lessons about loving and caring for others. They will see the example of a mom and dad who are doing their best to love and guide their family.

They will also see a leader that they want to follow.

LEADING TIP #5:
When you are a personhood leader, you won't have to make your kids follow you. They will want to.

Consider:

A personhood leader is one whose way of living inspires others to follow. What is one thing you can do in each of the three areas (i.e., connect, inspire, live) that will help you become the kind of leader your kids will want to follow?

Conclusion

We have covered a lot of territory with these eight tools, which I hope has been helpful to you. If you are anything like me, you will need to refer back to sections and chapters from time to time to keep these practical ideas fresh in your mind. The tips from each chapter are so important and can have such a powerful impact on your kids and family that I have put them together in the section that follows, and you may copy these tips for your easy reference.

If by chance you are wondering where to begin with all this, we've developed a **free parenting assessment** that will help you identify which of the eight parenting skills you are strongest in . . . and which areas you may need a little boost. It's a great way to prioritize how you can begin to apply the tools you've just learned and continue to love your kids well.

To take this short and insightful assessment,
visit www.8simpletools.com.

Summary of Tips

TALKING

Tip #1: Your communication style with your kids is REALLY, REALLY important. Not their communication style. Yours.

Tip #2: If you are not sure what to say, a brief pause can make all the difference between wise words and hurtful ones.

Tip #3: When you initiate conversations with your kids, it shows them that at that moment, you are more interested in them than in anything else.

Tip #4: When you are an easy-to-listen-to parent, your kids will be more open to the important lessons you want to teach.

Tip #5: When your conversations are like a friendly game of catch, everyone will want to be involved.

LISTENING

Tip #1: Listening first will always help you respond more wisely than if you had talked first.

Tip #2: When you listen to understand, your kids will want to unload their trucks in your zone on a regular basis.

Tip #3: If you want your kids to be comfortable talking to you, make sure they get plenty of opportunity to practice.

Tip #4: When you remember that everything your kids share with you is a diamond, you will want to listen to every single word.

Tip #5: When you listen with your entire body, it shows your kids that their thoughts and feelings are VALUABLE to you, which means that THEY are valuable to you.

INFLUENCING

Tip #1: When you remember who your kids really are, you can help them discover the gifts God has placed inside them.

Tip #2: Your words show your kids who you think they are, which shapes who they think they are. Use them wisely.

Tip #3: Your words can be a fountain of life to your kids.

Tip #4: Your kids are God's gold nuggets. The question is: Are you looking for the gold or the dirt?

Tip #5: Your kids don't just have a negative behavior to stop, they have an important lesson to learn.

CONNECTING

Tip #1: Warm physical touch communicates to your kids that you love them and want to be close to them.

Tip #2: Close relationships need quality interactions on a regular basis if you want them to stay close.

Tip #3: When you get into your child's world, they know you are doing it because you love them.

Tip #4: Learning together creates shared experiences and memories in a way that you and your kids will treasure for a lifetime.

Tip #5: A regular family time is one of the most powerful tools you can use to build a close and connected family.

TEACHING

Tip #1: When you follow the Family Respect Rule and teach it to your kids, your family will never be the same.

Tip #2: Practicing positive behavior together helps your kids develop good habits to replace the bad ones.

Tip #3: Flexible thinking will help your kids treat others the way they would like to be treated in any situation.

Tip #4: Every problem has one or more good solutions. Your kids can learn to find them.

Tip #5: An empathic response can open the door to mutual problem-solving and turn a situation around.

ENCOURAGING

Tip #1: Consistently pointing out positive behavior is a powerful way to transform your child's habits.

Tip #2: When you point out your kids' positive traits each day, you help them see the person God is helping them become.

Tip #3: When you point out the positive behavior and traits of all your kids on a regular basis, you create an encouraging family atmosphere where good habits and strong relationships can grow.

Tip #4: When kids learn to look past their failures, they will learn that God can bring something good out of any situation.

Tip #5: When you help your kids remember their good choices, it encourages them to make even more.

CORRECTING

Tip #1: Using parent flexible thoughts will help you focus on your job, stay in control of your emotions, and teach the right lessons, the right way.

Tip #2: Your choice of words can help your kids bounce back from a bad day or difficult situation.

Tip #3: A quick response will help your kids learn that negative choices get them nowhere. Fast.

Tip #4: The only way to make the fun circle go up is making the respect circle go up first.

Tip #5: Your correction style will open your kids up or shut them down to the lessons God wants them to learn from you.

LEADING

Tip #1: Kids learn by watching, and your example is the thing they will watch the most.

Tip #2: When you live your faith with your kids, you are writing God's commands on the doorframes of their hearts.

Tip #3: When your kids see you handle situations the right way, it makes it easier for them to do the same.

Tip #4: Showing your kids how to do wrong right is one of the most important lessons they will ever learn.

Tip #5: When you are a personhood leader, you won't have to make your kids follow you. They will want to.

NOTES

Introduction
1. Proverbs 14:15

Tool #1: Talking
1. Galatians 5:22–23
2. Proverbs 12:18

Tool #2: Listening
1. Proverbs 18:13
2. Luke 6:31
3. For example, *101 Conversation Starters for Families* by Gary Chapman and Ramon Presson is a good resource.

Tool #3: Influencing
1. Proverbs 18:21
2. Ephesians 2:10
3. Luke 6:31
4. Proverbs 10:11 (1984 version NIV)

Tool #4: Connecting
1. 1 Peter 2:17
2. Philippians 2:4
3. My book *Keep the Siblings, Lose the Rivalry* includes fifteen family time discussion guides that focus on skills for helping siblings get along better. Yes, you do need it.

Tool #5: Teaching
1. Luke 6:31
2. I have previously written about the Family Respect Rule in my book *Keep the Siblings, Lose the Rivalry* (Zondervan).
3. Ephesians 4:23
4. For a more detailed approach to teaching flexible thoughts, you can read my

ebook *Flexible Kids: Teach kids to handle the ups and downs of life—without getting bent out of shape.*

5. You may also enjoy playing The Flexible Thinking Game with your kids. It is a fun game designed to help kids practice flexible thinking. You can learn more about it at www.drtodd.net.

6. Proverbs 14:8

Tool #6: Encouraging

1. Hebrews 3:13
2. Ephesians 2:10
3. Galatians 5:22–23
4. Romans 8:28
5. Psalms 44; 78; Romans 1; 1 Corinthians 10; Hebrews 11

Tool #7: Correcting

1. My ebook *Raising Flexible Kids* contains instructions for Flexible Sentence Writing and completing Flexible Thinking Practice Sheets. Send one to your friends, then your kids will have nicer kids to play with.
2. Proverbs 19:18; 22:6
3. Luke 6:31
4. Proverbs 3:13–18
5. Galatians 5:22–23

Tool #8: Leading

1. 1 Corinthians 11:1
2. 1 Peter 5:7
3. James 1:27
4. 1 John 1:8–9
5. Proverbs 22:6
6. John Maxwell, *Developing the Leader Within You* (Nashville: Thomas Nelson, 2005).

Acknowledgments

This book is born out of the efforts of many wonderful and talented people. Jill, Megan, Brenda, and the entire Hearts at Home team have made wonderful contributions to this project and are always full of fun and mischief at the many Hearts at Home conferences I have had the privilege of participating in over the years.

John, Zack, Pam, and the team at Moody have been great to work with and full of creative ideas for which I am most grateful.

Thanks to Sandra Bishop at Transatlantic Agency for her invaluable help with all the details.

My wife and boys, of course, deserve much thanks for their patience and for allowing me to include portions of their lives in the pages of this book.

Finally, I must thank the thousands of Hearts at Home moms I have interacted with over the years, through both workshops and face-to-face discussions. These moms are beyond inspirational in their efforts to enrich their marriages and families and are no doubt an amazing blessing to the children God has entrusted them with.

The Go-To Place for Moms

Hearts at Home's mission is to encourage, educate, and equip every mom in every season of motherhood using Christian values to strengthen families. Founded in 1993, Hearts at Home offers a variety of resources and events to assist women in their roles as wives and mothers.

Hearts at Home is designed to provide you with ongoing education and encouragement in your journey of motherhood. In addition to this book, our resources include the Heartbeat Radio Program and our extensive Hearts at Home website, blog, and eCommunity. We also offer a monthly free eNewsletter called Hearts On-The-Go as well as daily encouragement on Facebook and Twitter.

Additionally, Hearts at Home conference events make a great getaway for individuals, moms' groups, or for enjoying time with that special friend, sister, or sister-in-law. The regional conferences, attended by more than ten thousand women each year, provide a unique, affordable, and highly encouraging weekend for any mom in any season of motherhood.

Hearts at Home
1509 N. Clinton Blvd.
Bloomington, IL 61702
Phone: (309) 828–MOMS
E-mail: hearts@hearts-at-home.org
Web: www.hearts-at-home.org

FREE PARENTING ASSESSMENT

Based on *8 Simple Tools for Raising Great Kids*!

We've developed a free parenting assessment that will help you identify which of the eight parenting skills you are strongest in . . . and which areas you may need a little boost.

Discover the small things you can do as a parent that will make a huge difference in your child's life. To take the assessment, visit **www.8simpletools.com**.

WWW.8SIMPLETOOLS.COM

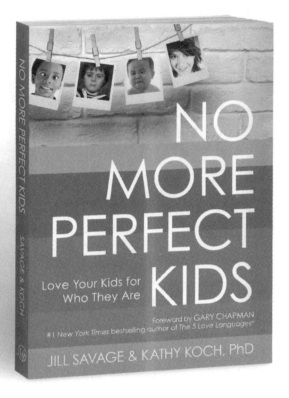

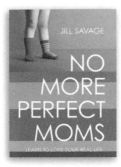

NO MORE PERFECT MOMS
Learn to Love Your Real Life

There is simply no such thing as a perfect mom. And there are no such things as perfect kids, perfect homes, perfect bodies, perfect marriages, or even perfect meals. With refreshing honesty, author Jill Savage exposes some of her own parental shortcomings with the goal of helping mothers everywhere shelve their desires for perfection along with their insecurities of not measuring up to other moms.

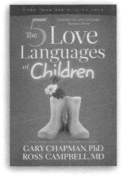

The 5 Love Languages of Children

Not only will Dr. Gary Chapman and Dr. Ross Campbell help you discover your child's love language, but you'll also learn how the love languages can help you discipline more effectively, build a foundation of unconditional love for your child, and understand the link between successful learning and the love languages.

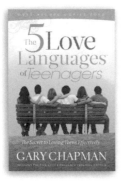

The 5 Love Languages of Teenagers
The Secret to Loving Teens Effectively

It's easy to tell when a teenager wants to be loved. Getting the message across is another matter entirely. In addition to the obvious generation gap, many parents and children face a sort of language barrier as well. The 5 Love languages of Teenagers is an invaluable tool for analyzing a teen's love language and expressing your affections in an effective way. The search for love in a teenager's life can lead to disastrous results. But if you can speak the right language, the difference can seem miraculous.

AVAILABLE WHEREVER BOOKS ARE SOLD.

IMPRO ... **RRIAGES**
... ONE LANGUAGE AT A TIME.

OVER
10 MILLION
SOLD!

ALL NEW &
REVISED!

NEW LOOK • NEW SIZE • NEW UPDATES

The 5 Love Languages® has transformed countless relationships. Its ideas are simple and conveyed with clarity and humor, making this book practical as it is personable. You'll be inspired by real-life stories and encouraged by its commonsense approach. Reading this book feels like taking a walk with a wise friend. Applying it will forever change your relationship—starting *today*.

WWW.5LOVELANGUAGES.COM